Rest for the Fortunate

Rest for the Fortunate
The Extraordinary Practice of Nyungne:
Its History, Meaning, and Benefits

by
Bardor Tulku Rinpoche

translated by
Lama Yeshe Gyamtso

Rinchen Publications
Kingston, New York USA

Published by
Rinchen, Inc.
20 John St.
Kingston, NY 12401
tel: (845) 331-5069
www.rinchen.com

Text: © 2004 Karma Triyana Dharmachakra
All Rights Reserved
Cover: © 2004 Rinchen Publications
All Rights Reserved
Line Drawing of 1000-Armed Chenrezig:
© Wendy Harding
All Rights Reserved
Printed in the USA

ISBN: 0-97145-543-0

Contents

Preface and Acknowledgements ... *i*

Introduction

Buddha Nature and the Nyungne Practice ... 1
Establishing the Proper Motivation
  for Study and Practice ... 4
Princess Lakshminkara and
  the Beginning of the Nyungne Tradition ... 5
A Brief Introduction to the Eight Vows ... 12
Taking on the Commitment of the Vows ... 15
Recitation of the Actual Vows ... 21
The Benefits of Observing the Vows ... 26
The Benefits of the Nyungne Practice Itself ... 27
The Benefits and Significance of Reciting
  the Dharanis and Mantra ... 34
Questions and Answers ... 39

Rest for the Fortunate

The Title, Subtitle, and Invocation ... 43

Part One

Introduction ... 47
Taking and Keeping the Vows
  According to the Hinayana ... 48
The Shortcomings of Not Keeping the Vows
  According to the Hinayana ... 50
The Benefits of Keeping the Vows
  According to the Hinayana ... 52
The Benefits of Keeping the Vows for One Day ... 55
Taking and Keeping the Vows
  According to the Mahayana ... 57
The Shortcomings of Not Keeping the Vows
  According to the Mahayana ... 63
The Benefits of Keeping the Vows
  According to the Mahayana ... 64
Taking and Keeping the Vows
  According to the Vajrayana ... 65
The Shortcomings of Not Keeping the Vajrayana Vows
  and Ritual Requirements ... 69

The Benefits of Keeping the Vows
   According to the Vajrayana . . . 70
Instructions and Benefits of Keeping One Seat . . . 72
Auspicious Months and Days to Do the Practice . . . 74
Some Personal Advice . . . 81
Questions and Answers . . . 84

PART TWO
   The Qualities of Chenrezig . . . 104
   The Tradition and Practice of Nyungne . . . 107
   Nyungne in the Context of the Buddhist Vehicles . . . 107
   The Lineage of Nyungne . . . 108
   When and How to Practice Nyungne . . . 129
   Further Statements on the Benefits of Nyungne . . . 130
   Chenrezig's Statements
      on the Benefits of Nyungne . . . 130
   The Benefits of Reciting or
      Recollecting the Name of Chenrezig . . . 133
   The Vajrayana Aspects of the Benefits . . . 136
   The Benefits of the Dharanis . . . 137
   The Benefits of *Om Mani Peme Hung* . . . 143
   The Benefits of Some Additional Dharanis . . . 145
   The Benefits of the Practice Ritual . . . 150
   The Benefits of the Generation
      and Completion Stages . . . 153
   The Commitments of the Nyungne Practice . . . 156

PART THREE:
   "AN IMPORTANT DIGRESSION" . . . 159

PREPARING FOR DEATH AND THE BARDO STATES
   Introduction . . . 171
   The Bardo Teachings of Guru Rinpoche . . . 176
   The Bardo of Dying:
      Dissolution and the Four Wisdoms . . . 178
   The Bardo of Dharmata:
      The Peaceful and Wrathful Deities . . . 184
   The Bardo of Becoming: The Journey of the Consciousness . . . 188
   Taking a Positive Rebirth . . . 193
   Questions and Answers . . . 197
   Rinpoche's Conclusion . . . 215

PREFACE

This book provides an essential background, explanation, and inspiration for anyone interested in one of the most powerful practice traditions of Tibetan Buddhism, the *nyungne*. The literal meaning of nyungne (pronounced NYUNG NAY) is "abiding in the fast." Fasting is indeed an important part of nyungne but, as you will see, it is only one feature of this rich and complex practice. In fact, nyungne effectively integrates the complete three-yana system of Tibetan Buddhism in a two-day retreat format. Practitioners take on temporary ordination by observing a strict set of vows from the tradition of individual liberation (hinayana). They generate the supreme altruistic motivation of *bodhicitta* as the internal basis for practice (mahayana). They also perform the liturgy, mantras, visualizations, and ritual observances of 1000-Armed Chenrezig from the kriya tantric tradition (vajrayana). *Rest for the Fortunate* gives a thorough explanation of the meaning of nyungne in the context of all these dimensions of Buddhism.

Another important aspect of the book is a presentation of the life stories of the main holders of the nyungne lineage. The lineage history begins with Princess Lakshminkara in ancient India, and continues up to Gyalsay Togmay (author of the famous *Thirty-Seven Practices of the Bodhisattvas*) who transmitted the nyungne so widely that it became part of all four major Tibetan lineages, and continues to this day. These stories are of great inspiration as we learn how they dedicated themselves completely and purely to practice, the great adversity they overcame, and the tremendous power of the practice in their lives.

Finally, *Rest for the Fortunate* is replete with traditional explanations of the effectiveness of nyungne practice. There are many stories of people who purified extremely negative karmic accumulations, overcame serious illness, and completely transformed themselves through this practice.

Preface and Acknowledgments

As well, there are extensive scriptural references from the sutras and tantras on the power of the vows, the mahayana motivation, the blessings of Chenrezig, and the mantras of the nyungne practice.

This book is not, however, a full set of practice instructions on nyungne. Traditionally, one would obtain such instructions in person from someone qualified to explain the details of the practice. That is still the best way to get instruction, especially since many traditions of nyungne exist, and some details differ. However, there are two resources I would like to mention. First is a complete explanation of the 1000-Armed Chenrezig sadhana (the main liturgy of the nyungne) which was given by Ven. Khenpo Karthar Rinpoche, Abbot of Karma Triyana Dharmachakra Monastery (KTD), in 1995. This teaching has been transcribed, but not yet edited. Second, Lama Tashi Dhöndrup, a Kagyu lama known for his meticulous knowledge of ritual detail, gave many hours of instruction on nyungne at KTD in the fall of 2002. These talks were videotaped, and they include instruction on the sequence of prayers, melodies for the liturgies, playing the musical instruments, and many other practical points. If there is sufficient interest and support for both these teachings, we can make them available.

The teaching on dying, death, and bardo at the end of the book was included here by Bardor Tulku Rinpoche because, quite simply, it is something that he, in his compassion, wants us to have. Though we normally would like to think of the benefits of meditation in terms of inner peace, happiness, and well-being in this life, the Buddhist teachings always emphasize that someday we must each face death. The Tibetan tradition in particular is very rich in instructions on working with the process of dying and the period after death in order to bring about a profound spiritual outcome. Bardor Tulku presents a special teaching from Guru Rinpoche (Padmasambhava) which discusses the bardo states in an especially lucid and helpful way.

A note about footnotes: All the footnotes in the text were written by the editors, except those marked [BTR] which are material given by Bardor Tulku Rinpoche in the question and answer sessions, which the editors thought would be more helpful in footnote form.

ACKNOWLEDGMENTS

Many people have generously contributed their skills and resources to this book. It represents but a tiny sliver of the teaching activity of Bardor Tulku Rinpoche, and his formal teaching is only one component of his tireless activity for His Holiness the Karmapa and for sentient beings. As well, we are so very fortunate to have such high caliber translation work by Lama Yeshe Gyamtso, who was also very helpful in answering the inevitable questions that come up in ironing out all the details in a text like this.

The teachings that make up this book were given in a series of seminars at centers across the country. The teachings that are the source of the first section of the book were given at Tampa Karma Thegsum Chöling (KTC) in the winter of 2001. Then the complete teaching on the traditional text *Rest for the Fortunate* was given in the fall of 2001 starting at Albany KTC and continuing at centers in Columbus, Ann Arbor, Chicago; Hay River, Wisconsin; and Ames, Iowa. The bardo teachings that conclude the book were given at Hartford, Connecticut KTC in September 1999. I am grateful to the center members who carefully recorded these teachings and forwarded them to KTD for transcription. Julie Neuharth, then KTC coordinator at KTD, was very helpful in this process.

The transcription of this material was also a large job. Ani Sherab Wangmo transcribed the first section of the book, and her work was sponsored by a job training program of the Lighthouse Foundation. I thank the Foundation, and Shelly Armory for coordinating that sponsorship. Tara

Preface and Acknowledgments

Steele transcribed the teachings on the Tibetan text *Rest for the Fortunate* that make up the bulk of this book. I am extremely grateful to her for generously taking time to do this despite her many commitments as a staff member of KTD at that time. The bardo teachings were kindly transcribed by Linda Duncan.

Concerning editing of *Rest for the Fortunate*, I was the primary editor through its various versions, but had the help of two very fine assistants. Karma Sonam Drolma (who also edited Rinchen's recent *The Wish-Fulfilling Wheel* by Khenpo Karthar Rinpoche) was incredibly generous with her time in reading the manuscript not once but twice, and making a huge contribution to its clarity of expression, as well as very helpful suggestions on structure and presentation. Florence Wetzel has also read the text several times and brought to the work a very fine eye for language and meaning, along with paying patient attention to the detailed structure of *Rest for the Fortunate*. Although the work of Florence and Drolma is largely the basis for the quality of the editorial work, I made all the final editorial decisions and take full responsibility for any errors or shortcomings.

The cover was designed and executed by Louise Light, and I want to thank her not just for producing yet another stunning design job for Rinchen Publications, but for her patience and generosity over the rather long period it took to bring the overall project to completion. The photograph used in the cover was most kindly produced by Peter Van Deurzen of KTD's Namse Bangdzo Bookstore, using a wonderful statue of 1000-Armed Chenrezig, one of the many he imports from Nepal.

The line drawing of 1000-Armed Chenrezig at the front of the book was drawn specially for this project by Wendy Harding. When done in the traditional manner by a trained artist such as Wendy, a drawing of this kind is a tremendous amount of work. In this case, each of the 1000 hands (and the eyes on each hand) were drawn individually. The original is in a much larger size than it appears in the book and is truly amazing. If there is interest among the readership of this book, Wendy has indicated her willingness to make available larger-size reproductions of her drawing. These would be excellent both as visualization aids and as framable dharma art. The drawing was scanned for the book by Sherry Williams of Oxygen Design.

At a personal level, I am very grateful to Ilfra Halley for her support and kindness in so many ways over the time I have been working on this project. I also extend my thanks to my friend and dharma brother Cralle Hall, whose spiritual and financial backing of Rinchen has been present from the beginning and still continues. I also thank my mother, Dr. Alice McCarthy, and my father and his wife, Walter and Linda McCarthy, for all their help and love over the years, and in particular for financial support of Rinchen Publications.

Finally, the production of this book has been made possible by a group of very generous donors who have sponsored a large portion of the printing. I am very grateful to them, not only for practicing the traditional and highly meritorious custom of sponsoring Dharma books for distribution, but also for their patience and kindness in the long period it took to bring the book to completion.

These teachings embody great blessings in so many ways. There are those of the teacher, Bardor Tulku Rinpoche, who has made them available to us; there are the blessings of the great Kagyu lineage holder, the Ninth Situ Rinpoche, who composed the traditional text; there are the blessings of the peerless lineage holders of nyungne, and the inherent blessings of the nyungne itself. Since this is so, I am confident that *Rest for the Fortunate* will be the doorway for many to the practice of nyungne and its supreme benefits.

David McCarthy
President, Rinchen Publications
Kingston, New York

INTRODUCTION

Buddha Nature and the Nyungne Practice

The Buddha taught that the basic nature of each and every being is completely perfect and always has been. This basic nature is identical to that of a buddha. Therefore all beings have, as their very nature, the capacity for full awakening or buddhahood. If our basic nature is perfect, then why is it that we experience confusion and suffering, and why do we wander in the state of cyclic existence?[1] The Buddhist view is that there are two factors involved in this negative cycle: wrongdoing and mental obscuration. Wrongdoing is anything we do with our body, speech, or mind that is harmful. When we do something that is harmful, that further obscures our minds, so obscuration is the result of wrongdoing. Wrongdoing and the resulting obscurations cause us to suffer and wander in cyclic existence.

The relationship between our basic nature and our obscurations is similar to the following analogy: when the sun is in the sky it is always very bright—in fact, its brilliance is so great that it can dispel all darkness. However, when there are clouds the sun's brilliance appears to have diminished. Also, when night comes as the earth turns on its axis each day, the sun seems to disappear completely. Of course, in both these cases the sun itself is unaffected. Its light has not dimmed; its nature has not changed—and certainly it has not gone away. Nevertheless, the obscuration by the clouds or the earth at night definitely affects how we perceive it.

---

1. Cyclic existence (*samsara* in Sanskrit) is one of the core concepts of Buddhism. The fundamental characteristics of samsara are confusion and suffering. It is the opposite of *nirvana*. Under the influence of fundamental ignorance, beings are caught in an ongoing cycle of birth, death, and rebirth through a process known as interdependent origination. Cyclic existence can only end for a being when that being becomes enlightened.

The sun in this analogy is similar to our basic nature — our buddha nature. It is flawless and full of qualities as brilliant as the sun. It is in every way identical to the basic nature of a buddha. It is not affected, corrupted, or destroyed by our negative mental patterns or obscurations. Nevertheless, just like the sun, although our basic nature cannot be affected in any way by obscurations, it *can* be concealed. Like the clouds that obscure the sun's light, our wrongdoings and obscurations conceal or obscure the light of our own basic nature. Though they obscure our basic nature, however, they do not affect it in any way. Our basic nature remains absolutely pure and utterly perfect. Therefore the obscurations are considered to be incidental to our inherent buddha nature. For that reason they can be removed.

If you were to ask how the obscurations arise in the first place, the answer is that it all begins with the mind failing to recognize itself. We call this ignorance. In essence, the Buddhist spiritual path is about gradually overcoming this ignorance so that we can ultimately recognize the true nature of mind. The nyungne practice combines all the main types of training that Buddhists have traditionally undertaken in their practice of this path in order to attain this goal. Much of what we will cover in this book is about the benefits of the nyungne practice. As you will see, they are amazing.

Nyungne is a practice of the eleven-faced, thousand-armed form of Chenrezig *(Avalokiteshvara)*. Chenrezig is the embodiment of all the love and compassion of all buddhas of the past, present, and future in the form of a bodhisattva. By his very nature, therefore, he is a great bodhisattva who benefits all beings continually. For this reason Chenrezig is regarded as the source of all blessings. We have all accumulated a great deal of obscurations in our countless lifetimes in cyclic existence. However, by meditating on the form of Chenrezig, repeating the mantra of Chenrezig, and resting in meditation upon Chenrezig, we can purify all of these obscurations and all of our wrongdoings of body, speech, and mind.

Through this practice we can also accomplish what are called the two attainments, or *siddhis*. The first of these, common attainment, means achieving such benefits as a fortunate rebirth, longevity, well-being, and so forth. The second is called supreme attainment. This is the ultimate fruition, which is buddhahood.

This practice of Chenrezig involves meditating on love and compassion for all beings. By meditating upon this deity, it is possible to develop extraordinary love and compassion. In doing so, you will gradually become more and more like him and develop the genuine ability to benefit others.

Of course, most of us already possess some degree of love and compassion. But usually our love and compassion is imperfect and limited. That is to say, it is partial, which means that we usually love some and not others. In addition, even when we love someone it is not unusual for us to stop loving that person, and for that feeling to change into dislike or even hatred. Our innate love and compassion is limited because we are affected by the negative mental patterns and obscurations that we have accumulated throughout beginningless time as we have wandered in cyclic existence under the power of ignorance. The practice of meditating on the Bodhisattva Chenrezig is a way to purify or remove this ignorance and these negative mental patterns and thereby reveal our own innate buddha nature, which is the essence of love, compassion, and bodhicitta.[2]

All beings wish to achieve happiness and avoid suffering, but in most cases they lack a correct understanding of what constitutes the causes of happiness and the causes of suffering. Therefore happiness is rare and most beings experience a great deal of suffering. The practice of Chenrezig enables us to gradually eradicate the causes of suffering and bring about the causes of happiness, both for ourselves and for others.

---

2. Bodhicitta is a central principle of mahayana Buddhism. In its relative aspect, it is both the aspiration and the activity one undertakes to achieve supreme enlightenment such that all beings without exception will achieve supreme enlightenment. The absolute aspect of bodhicitta is the enlightened mind itself.

The special and unique quality of the nyungne practice is that it is greatly beneficial for people who are very busy, particularly householders who can only spare a day or two at a time for intensive practice. Because the practice is so powerful, they can accomplish a tremendous amount even in one or two days.

Finally, nyungne is an especially significant practice for those who are practitioners of the Karma Kagyu tradition because our guru, the Gyalwa Karmapa, is the continuous incarnation among us of the Bodhisattva Chenrezig.

Establishing the Proper Motivation for Study and Practice

This teaching and the practice it describes are from the mahayana tradition of Buddhism. In the mahayana we aspire not only for our own enlightenment but for the enlightenment of all beings. Therefore it is traditional at the beginning of a mahayana teaching for the teacher to remind the students of this, and to ask them to keep this motivation firmly in mind while listening to the teaching. Therefore I would like to ask you to do so as you are reading and studying this book. Please read it with the motivation of bodhicitta. This means having the thought, "I am studying the genuine Dharma so that I can establish each and every being throughout space in a state of perfect and manifest awakening." With this attitude, study this teaching not only for your own benefit, but in order to free all beings from suffering and establish them in a state of permanent happiness. Make the aspiration and intention to properly receive the profound, genuine Dharma and put it into practice.

This motivation is essential for practitioners of the mahayana when practicing or receiving any instruction, transmission, or empowerment. If you maintain this outlook as you study this book, you will be participating from the very beginning in the supreme compassion of bodhicitta, which provides the profound and sacred environment for the practice of nyungne.

Princess Lakshminkara and the Beginning of the Nyungne Tradition

As an introduction to the practice and to inspire confidence and enthusiasm in the study and practice of nyungne, we will begin by talking about the life story of the founder of the nyungne tradition, Lakshminkara, who is also known as Gelongma Palmo.

In ancient times there was a kingdom known as Uddiyana. It is believed that this was roughly in the same area as present-day Afghanistan. The king of Uddiyana was named Indrabhuti, and one of his children was the princess Lakshminkara. From a very early age she was quite well known in that part of the world because she was both extremely intelligent and extraordinarily beautiful. She was so special that all of the kings and noblemen throughout that region of India wanted to ask for her hand in marriage. However, she had no interest in being married or becoming the queen of a kingdom. She recognized that samsara is nothing but suffering and that everything except the practice of the genuine Dharma is meaningless. Therefore at the age of twelve, before any of her suitors succeeded in winning her in marriage, she took monastic ordination. After her ordination she was known as Gelongma Palmo.

She quickly became learned in all five traditional areas of learning and especially in the spiritual teachings of Buddhism. Before much time had passed, however, the residue of her previous negative karma ripened and she was stricken with leprosy. Her body became completely covered with ulcerated sores like a flower stricken with blight. The sores began leaking lymph and her face became completely distorted and wrinkled and twisted. Her pain was unbearable, and kept getting worse. Finally, from her body came a continual stream of blood and pus. The bones in her wrists decayed to the point where she could not use her hands, and because of that she was unable to feed herself any longer. She could only lie on the ground like an animal and get food and drink by sticking her face into containers of easily digestible food and water that were placed before her.

Because there was much fear of leprosy at that time, the people in the kingdom sent her to live in a grass hut outside the citadel. One night, while she was living there in misery, she dreamed about her father, King Indrabhuti. In the dream, he was holding a crystal vase. He said to her, "This is the cleansing water of the great compassionate one, Chenrezig. Do not be miserable, because through this illness you will quickly attain supreme siddhi. The eleven-faced form of Chenrezig is the embodiment of all buddhas. Pray to him." With these words, he washed her with the water from the vase, pouring it over her. In the dream her suffering was considerably reduced, and her body and mind became more at ease.

When she awoke the next morning she felt slightly better physically and therefore was less disturbed in her mind. Thus she was able to begin reciting the six-syllable mantra of Chenrezig, *om mani peme hung*,[3] as she had been instructed in her dream. After reciting it for a time, the bones in her left wrist began to heal. Finally, she was able to feed herself again, but only with her left hand.

From that point onward she practiced more and more intensely. She would recite the six-syllable mantra *om mani peme hung* all day, and all night she would recite the dharani of the eleven-faced form of Chenrezig. (The dharani is the longer mantra in the nyungne practice.) After six months

---

3. This spelling is according to the Tibetan pronunciation of the mantra. The word *peme* sounds like "peh may" and the last syllable sounds like "hoong." The Sanskrit spelling and pronunciation is *om mani padme hum*.

of this she began to feel discouraged, and one morning she thought, "No matter how much they practice a deity, someone in my position will never be able to realize him. I would be better off dead." Thinking that, she went to sleep. She immediately had a dream in which the Bodhisattva Manjushri appeared. He said to her, "Go to the temple of Shenpal, and if you live there and meditate on the Bodhisattva Chenrezig for five years you will achieve the same state of realization as Tara and will be able to benefit beings immeasurably." Then in the dream he placed an amrita pill on her tongue and disappeared like a rainbow dissolving into the sky.

From that point onward, she felt tremendous loving-kindness and compassion. Deciding to do as she had been instructed in the dream, she traveled to the temple while praying continuously to Chenrezig. On the way there, several carnivorous animals and poisonous snakes threatened her. Whenever this occurred she supplicated Chenrezig and they just disappeared. Seven *mamos*,[4] in the form of mantrikas, assisted her on her journey as protectors. Finally, two wisdom dakinis appeared and, supporting her on a seat of cotton (it was almost like a stretcher), they transported her the final distance to the temple.

When she reached the temple she asked the monks there which of them was the custodian of the temple. One of them said he was, and she said, "I have come here to meet the Great Compassionate One." This was a temple of Chenrezig, and its central image was a statue of the eleven-faced, thousand-armed form of the deity. She requested that she be allowed to live in the temple and practice directly in front of the statue. The custodian said to her, "Because of your

---

4. Mamos are a broad class of female worldly deities, and are often emanations of some more exalted feminine principle. Most of the time they appear in wrathful form as angry or ugly women, but they can also manifest in beautiful forms. They often act as protectors of the Dharma.

illness I cannot allow you to live inside the temple. You can live behind it and supplicate the statue from there."

Doing as he had instructed, she stayed out behind the temple and began praying continuously to the statue of Chenrezig. As she did this, the statue inside the temple miraculously began to rise up from its pedestal. When the custodian saw this, he immediately went to her and said, "Although you are a leper, you seem to have great power and great qualities, so I will allow you to live and practice inside the temple." She took her seat in front of the statue of the Eleven-Faced One and resolved not to leave until she obtained supreme siddhi (buddhahood). Having undertaken this firm commitment to exert herself in practice, she did not even think about food and drink. She simply ate and drank whatever she received. Throughout day and night she practiced the meditation on Eleven-Faced Chenrezig one-pointedly.

At the end of a year the flesh of her body, which was completely covered with sores from the leprosy, was discarded like a snake shedding its old skin. All of the sores and everything simply fell off. Her body became just as healthy and beautiful as it had been before she was stricken with the disease. In fact, her appearance was even more beautiful than it had been before. All of her suffering, wrongdoing, and obscurations had been cleared away, and she obtained the first level *(bhumi*[5]*)* of bodhisattva realization. An inconceivable samadhi was born in her mind. The uplifted state of her mind was so powerful that whenever there was any obstacle created by Mara, simply through meditating on bodhicitta she could even cause the obstructer to become compassionate. Therefore all those who were looking for opportunities to distract or tempt her, such as the ten worldly protectors, were attracted to her and, through the power of her meditation on Chenrezig, became her helpers. In that way they were drawn in and bound by samaya

---

5. In the bodhisattva path there are ten stages or *bhumis* leading to complete enlightenment.

and became protectors of this practice. In particular, eight nagas promised to be Dharma protectors of this tradition.

On the first day of the fourth month (the month of Saga) she had a vision of Tara. On the eighth day of that month she had a vision of Amoghapasha (which is the kriya tantra form of Chenrezig) and all of the deities of kriya tantra.[6] On the fifteenth day, the full moon day, she had a vision of the eleven-faced, thousand-armed form of Chenrezig, and received his teachings directly. Through this, all 84,000 samadhis associated with all varieties of Dharma arose within her. At that time she attained the eighth bodhisattva bhumi.

Then she performed a nyungne for three months for the benefit of sentient beings. During this time she remained at the height of seven palm trees in the sky. She radiated innumerable rays of light from her body, at the tips of which were offering gods and goddesses. At that time she com-

---

6. In general, the kriya tantra is the first level of the four tantras. *Kriya* literally means action. The second level is called charya tantra. *Charya* means behavior. *Yoga* tantra is the third, and the fourth is called *anuttarayoga*, or highest yoga tantra. One way that the differences between the levels are traditionally presented is in terms of the degree to which the practice of the tantra involves external conduct as opposed to internal meditation. In kriya tantra the emphasis is on the actions (or kriyas) of ablution and external purity. In addition, no matter what form the meditation takes, there is a sense of considering yourself as inferior and the deity as superior. To clarify the difference, we will consider the third level, yoga tantra, next. It is called yoga tantra or the tantra of unification because there is an identification with the deity that is so strong — because there is no longer any sense of inferiority or superiority — that the external actions or kriyas of ablution and so forth are unimportant. The fourth level, anuttarayoga tantra, is beyond any kind of duality whatsoever between the practitioner and the deity. The second level, charya tantra, is a combination of the meditative practices of the yoga tantra with the ritual ablution of kriya tantra. [BTR]

posed the *Praise to Chenrezig* that is contained in the nyungne practice that we do in the Karma Kagyu tradition.

After this, Gelongma Palmo returned to the central region of India. She went to the capital of Uddiyana. There was a mahasiddha living there who was engaging in the conduct of a siddha, the conduct of yogic discipline.[7] She approached him for instruction and under his guidance entered into the dance of profound secret co-emergent great bliss. This means that she became a yogini. Through that she obtained the tenth bodhisattva level. She lived in Uddiyana as a mahasiddha exhibiting the conduct of a siddha of the secret mantrayana.[8] In fact, Lakshminkara is best known as one of 84 mahasiddhas.

At that point the people of Uddiyana, especially those in the capital region who had known her all her life, denigrated her because she was behaving like a mahasiddha, saying, "Well, it's nice that the bhikshuni (nun) has been cured of leprosy and she looks the way she looked before, but it is not nice that as soon as she was cured of leprosy she abandoned her monastic vows." In response, she went to the middle of the marketplace in the center of town and appeared to sever her own head from her neck with a knife. She then said, "If I have violated my moral commitments, may my head and body remain separate, but if my morality is pure, may they be joined as they were before." Having made that aspiration, her head popped up and landed right back on her neck and they were joined just as they had been before. When the people saw that, they were awestruck and realized that she must be a mahasiddha and a great yogini.

---

7. The conduct of yogic discipline may include unconventional behavior arising from the utter freedom of mind of a realized being.
8. The term mantrayana is synonymous with the terms vajrayana and tantrayana.

Rest for the Fortunate

After having gained acceptance in Uddiyana, she composed a ritual sadhana of nyungne. Through the practice of nyungne which began in Uddiyana under her supervision a great many people were established in ripening and liberation. Though it was initially known only in Uddiyana, eventually it became widespread throughout all of Buddhist India. Innumerable people in that country took it as their principal practice and achieved liberation through it.

It also spread to Tibet. Initially, when King Songtsen Gampo, who was an emanation of Chenrezig, first started to teach and propagate the Dharma, he encouraged all of his subjects to regularly undertake the eight vows of the nyungne. Five generations after that, the Dharma King Trisong Deutsen invited the great abbot Shantirakshita to formally establish the Buddha's teachings in Tibet. As is recorded in the records of that time and the biographies of Guru Rinpoche and others, Shantirakshita composed a ritual and liturgy for both the nyungne and the nyinay practices. In fact, according to the most extensive biography of Guru Rinpoche, on that occasion the king and several of his courtiers performed the nyinay[9] practice together.

Guru Rinpoche, who is known as "The Second Buddha from Uddiyana," was also active in the transmission of the nyungne tradition. In many of his hidden teachings *(termas)* he concealed nyungne practices of the tradition of Gelongma Palmo. From that time onward the nyungne practice became very widespread in Tibet. Many beings have accomplished complete liberation through taking it as their principal practice.

---

9. Nyinay is a one-day practice, whereas nyungne is a complete two-day practice with a specific liturgy. Nyungne literally means to remain or abide in a fast. Nyinay means to remain for a day. On the day that you undertake a nyinay, you would eat only one meal, but you can drink liquids throughout the day. If you do a nyungne it is like a nyinay on the first day, then on the second day you do not eat, drink, or talk.

Nyungne has been passed down through all of the schools of Tibetan Buddhism. The form of practice we do within the Karma Kagyu was introduced and made widespread by the eighth Karmapa, Mikyö Dorje. The blessings of the original source of this tradition are unimpaired. The river of empowerment is undiminished; the continuity of the profound practical instructions is unbroken, and the detailed explanation of the practice is undamaged. Therefore the true or ultimate lineage of the nyungne still exists and is still available. This lineage has never been harmed by broken samaya and therefore contains all the qualities that are necessary for a practice to bring about awakening. For this reason the instructions of nyungne are like the quintessence of the ambrosia of Dharma. We will continue with the history of the nyungne lineage in detail later in the book.

A Brief Introduction to the Eight Vows

In his great wisdom and compassion, the Buddha taught a vast variety of methods that lead to spiritual awakening. The practice of nyungne is a very special and powerful example of those methods. It is sometimes called "the fasting ritual," and is done in the context of the deity practice of Thousand-Armed Chenrezig. In addition, nyungne involves doing what is called the renewal and purification practice of the eight vows, and it is with the taking of those vows that the practice begins.

Buddhism is based in a very fundamental way on the idea of cause and result. As we see in the example of plant life in the natural world, what grows will always correspond to what was planted. In the same way, what we experience results from our actions. If you do something virtuous, you will experience happiness. If you do something negative, you will experience misery. Specifically, it is taught that rebirth in the higher realms and liberation can only come about as the result of the karma produced by the intentional observation of some kind of moral discipline. Thus the purpose of observing vows of moral discipline is to achieve rebirth in the higher realms and attain liberation.

We will begin our study of the practice with the vows. In looking at the vows, we will start with an overview of their context and purpose. This will include a detailed explanation of the words of the vows and what they refer to. It may be helpful to refer to the actual nyungne liturgy text as we go through this.

The class of practices that includes the nyungne is called renewal and purification, or *sojong* in Tibetan. About sojong practices in general, it was said by Guru Rinpoche:

> The function of such a practice is to renew or refresh all forms of virtue and to purify or remove all manner of wrongdoing. It is called renewal and purification because it renews or refreshes virtue and purifies and removes wrongdoing. That is why the sugatas *[the buddhas]* have taught this practice.

When you take the sojong vows, they function in two ways: (1) to renew your commitment to the training of Dharma (that is, your commitment to virtue), and (2) to purify whatever wrongdoing you have engaged in. In general, there are two different types of sojong practice. One is renewal and purification through shamata or tranquility meditation. The second type is called concordant renewal and purification, which is done through some form of ritual. The vows taken during nyungne practice are in the second category, that of concordant renewal and purification.

In addition, there are two types of concordant renewal and purification. One is what is called a timely or occasional sojong and the other is called a sojong of uncertain time. The timely sojong is one that must be done by fully ordained monastics twice a month around the time of the full and new moons. This is a ritual based on the *Pratimoksha Sutra* involving the renewal and purification of monastic ordination. The second type of renewal and purification can be done pretty much at any time, and is not a ritual requirement of monastic ordination. The vows of nyungne fall within that second category.

Then in the category of sojong that can be done at any time, there are two types, namely the hinayana and the mahayana forms.[10] Nyungne practice is of the mahayana form. The actual moral commitments that you take when you do a nyungne are eightfold. In the hinayana, these eight vows are a type of layperson's vows that are taken temporarily for a specific period of time. Since here they are practiced in the context of the bodhisattva vehicle (the mahayana), they are seen as part of the practice of abstention from wrongdoing which is one of the three aspects of the perfection *(paramita)* of morality *(shila* in Sanskrit, *tsultrim* in Tibetan). Thus they become part of the practice of the six perfections for a mahayana practitioner.

Taking vows and keeping them in the nyungne practice is done in conjunction with the generation stage[11] of Chenrezig

---

10. The word "yana" in Sanskrit means vehicle or path. Hinayana, mahayana, and vajrayana refer to the main categories of Buddhist practice as presented in the Tibetan tradition. Hinayana is mainly concerned with the liberation of oneself from samsara, whereas in mahayana and vajrayana (also called tantrayana or mantrayana) one takes on the commitment to achieve buddhahood for the purpose of bringing all sentient beings to a state of buddhahood. The intention and result of mahayana and vajrayana are the same, but vajrayana is distinguished by its wealth of special methods that can lead to rapid progress on the path.

11. The generation stage is one of the two stages of vajrayana meditation. In this stage, the practitioner develops and meditates on the visualization that is the focus of the practice. For example, in the nyungne practice, the generation stage involves the visualization of Thousand-Armed Chenrezig.

in accordance with the traditions of kriya tantra. Therefore they are essentially a form of kriya tantra austerity. Moral discipline as it is practiced in the nyungne is both an aspect of keeping the sojong commitments and an aspect of conduct in the sense of emulation. In undertaking these commitments you are saying, "I am emulating the behavior of all the buddhas and bodhisattvas of the past, and I am making the commitment to conduct myself in that way." This is in keeping with the fundamental meaning of *tsultrim*, which literally means "manner and rule" in Tibetan.

Taking on the Commitment of the Vows

There are two parts in the ritual used to take the vows: taking on the commitment of the vows, and recitation of the actual vows.

There are two ways to take the commitments to the vows and the vows themselves. They can be taken from a preceptor or lama, in which case the assembly repeats the words of the vows, a few words at a time, after the leader. The other way is that everyone can repeat the words together directly from the liturgy. This is commonly done if you have already received the vows from a teacher or if there is no teacher available when you are doing the nyungne practice.

In the first part, the particular vows are not specified. You repeat the words of the liturgy three times with your hands joined together at the heart and with your body in a kneeling position.

What follows is pretty much a word-by-word explanation of what you say when you take on the commitment to keep the vows during the nyungne practice. As you will see in the nyungne text, you recite certain phrases such as "just as all the arhats ...," "like a royal steed ...," "like an elephant ..." We will go over why you say these things and what they mean. You will see that the entire vow is phrased as an emulation of the buddhas and bodhisattvas.

The liturgy begins, "All buddhas and bodhisattvas who abide in the ten directions, please attend me." Buddhas are called tathagatas, which means "those who have gone like that." "Like that" refers to dharmata or suchness, the nature of all things. When we refer to buddhas, especially to the buddhas of the past (although this term does not only mean buddhas of the past), we often call them tathagatas. That is because they have realized the nature of all things. Therefore they have gone to a state that is concordant with that nature.

They are also called arhats. A buddha is not merely an arhat, but in this case the term arhat refers to the fact that a perfect samyaksambuddha (a term for a complete and perfect buddha) has conquered the four maras. The four maras are: (1) the mara which is kleshas or mental afflictions; (2) the mara which is skandhas[12] or aggregates; (3) the mara which

---

12. The term *skandha* is usually translated as aggregate. The aggregates are an inclusive list of all objects of knowledge which includes everything in samsara. They are called aggregates to show that each of these five aspects of experience is itself made up of many little bits. The five skandhas are: (1) form, (2) feeling (or sensation), (3) perception, (4) mental formation, and (5) consciousness. Form refers to all physical matter, anything that has physical form. That includes your body, your senses, and all the objects of the senses. Sensation includes all your sensations, pleasant, unpleasant, and neutral. In the same way, perception is all of the things that you perceive. Mental formations include all of your thoughts. Consciousness includes the mind that generates those thoughts. As the name *aggregate* would imply, there are many, many divisions within each of these. For example, in terms of form there are usually what are called the four causal forms (the four elements) as well as the eleven resultant forms, which are the five sense organs, the five sense objects, and imperceptible forms. [BTR]

is death; and (4) the mara which is called "the child of the gods" and which means, in a psychological sense, addiction to that which is pleasant.[13]

In addition to this, buddhas have perfectly completed all qualities of freedom or abandonment. This means they have accomplished the abandonment of ignorance and all that comes from ignorance, and have attained realization. They have realized the true nature of things, which comes about upon the abandonment of ignorance. Therefore they have awakened from the thick sleep of ignorance. This is the fundamental meaning of the word *buddha*: it means to be awake. In that awakening, all things that are to be known are clear in their minds. Therefore they are not only awakened, but their minds have fully expanded or blossomed like a lotus. This means they have achieved the full capacity of the mind to know. That is why the Sanskrit word *buddha* is translated into Tibetan with the word *sangye*. The first syllable, *sang*, means purified, and the second syllable, *gye*, means expanded or bloomed.

---

13. Basically the problem with desiring that which is pleasant is that strong attachment to pleasure becomes a cause for further rebirth in samsara. There is no way that you can achieve liberation from samsara without overcoming this strong attachment. There are two kinds of examples we can look to which show how to overcome this. King Indrabhuti exemplifies the first kind of example. While enjoying all the pleasures and splendors of being a king, he was nevertheless unstained by attachment. Another example of that is Lord Marpa. Viewed externally, such persons would seem to be as attached to pleasure as anyone else, but in fact they were not because their involvement in the pleasures of the senses was like a snake coiling itself into a knot. Any time a snake wants, it can uncoil itself. It does not have to be uncoiled by anything else. However, if you are unable to do that, your only other choice is to follow the example of the great masters of the Kadampa tradition, who directly attack attachment by focusing on and reversing whatever attachment they discover in themselves through radical renunciation. [BTR]

Legend tells us that chakravartins have a royal steed that will always bring the monarch who rides it home safely from battle regardless of how severely the steed itself is wounded. In the same way, buddhas are here said to be like the royal steed in the sense that they always perform benefit for others. They do not have any concern for their own welfare. That is the meaning of this reference to the royal steed in the nyungne liturgy. The buddhas always teach beings the path to liberation and omniscience.

Next in the liturgy it says " . . . like elephants." Without being asked, buddhas carry the great burden of benefiting all beings throughout space and teaching the unsurpassable Dharma. Therefore they are like elephants that can carry even the heaviest burden. Because they have achieved complete benefit for themselves in obtaining buddhahood, they have "done the deeds," which is the next phrase in the text. Various translations might say something like, "who have completed the action." Then, because they continue to actively benefit others, it next says, "who are doing what has to be done."

Because the buddhas have abandoned all karma and kleshas—in short, all obscurations—they have cast aside that burden. Therefore the next phrase is, "who have cast aside the burden." The text goes on, "who have perfectly obtained their own benefit." That is because they have obtained the state of nirvana. It continues, "who have completely exhausted all entrance into existence." This means that they have completely exhausted all the kleshas and inferior views that cause someone to remain in samsara.

The text continues, "They give the perfect dictates or commands." That means that the buddhas teach the Dharma that is virtuous in the beginning, middle, and end. Next it says, "Their minds are utterly liberated." This means that they are completely free from all the bonds of existence. Then it says, "They possess the discernment of excellent and perfect liberation." Because they are liberated from the bonds of existence they possess the wisdom that knows all things just as they are.

Next is, "just as they have done." "They" refers to all of those buddhas who possess all of those qualities and who, with the motivation of bodhicitta which wishes to establish all beings in the state of perfect awakening, have totally given up concern for their own welfare and have engaged in benefit for sentient beings. They "have done" so in order to temporarily establish beings in a state of higher rebirth and finally in a state of liberation.

The text further elaborates, "for the benefit of all beings, in order to liberate all beings, in order to free all beings from sickness," and so forth. "For the benefit of all beings" means that the buddhas have cast aside all concern for their own welfare in order to benefit all beings. The particular meaning of "for the benefit of all beings" here means to establish all beings in higher rebirth. "For the liberation of all beings" means to establish beings in a state of liberation from samsara.

The expression "to free all beings from sickness" is metaphoric. It refers to healing beings of the affliction of the kleshas, and in this case especially anger. Thus, when it says "to free all beings from sickness," it means to purify the anger of all sentient beings. The illness of the kleshas is far worse than physical illness because physical illness can at the most kill us once. It will not follow us from life to life. The illness of the kleshas has been following us life after life after life and kills us again and again.

Then it says, "to free them from starvation." That means the starvation which is the experience, cause, and result of greed. Then the liturgy says, "in order to complete the factors of awakening." This refers to the thirty-seven factors of awakening, which are the fourfold close placement of mindfulness, the four perfect abandonments, the four bases of miracles, the five strengths, the five powers, the seven factors of awakening, and the noble eightfold path.[14] In this way the liturgy clarifies our intention that all of these virtues be actualized.

Finally it says, "in order that unsurpassable and perfect complete awakening be obtained, just as all of these buddhas have undertaken the vows of renewal and purification (the eight vows), in the same way I, for the benefit of all beings, from this time until sunrise tomorrow undertake the same morality." Almost all of the above describes the virtues of the buddhas, which you aspire to emulate through taking the vows.

---

14. The fourfold close placement of mindfulness, the four perfect abandonments, the four bases of miracles, the five strengths, the five powers, the seven factors of awakening, and the noble eightfold path are all part of a rather extensive teaching that covers the entire path of awakening from a Dharma point of view. It is a description of the Buddhist path common to all vehicles. You will find it in the hinayana, the mahayana, and the vajrayana. It is broken down into what is known as the five paths, and those are further divided into what are known as the thirty-seven factors of awakening. These include the fourfold close placement of mindfulness, the fourfold perfect abandonments, the four miraculous bases, five strengths, five powers, seven factors of awakening, and the noble eightfold path. The first twelve (the first three groups of four) are the factors of awakening cultivated on the path of accumulation, which is the first of five paths. The five strengths and five powers are developed on the next of the five paths, that of juncture. The seven factors relate to the path of seeing, and the noble eightfold path occurs on the path of meditation. You can find descriptions of these in many texts. For example, there is a detailed teaching on this subject in Khenpo Karthar Rinpoche's book *Dharma Paths*. This is the principal description of the spiritual path for all Buddhist traditions. These factors are interpreted and represented differently in each tradition, but the nature of the path is the same. For example in the nyungne practice you visualize a palace in the frontal visualization. The palace has thirty-seven features that represent these thirty-seven factors of awakening. [BTR]

After three repetitions of this liturgy, you have completed the commitment to keep the vows. Thus far, the particular vows have not been specified.

Recitation of the Actual Vows

The second part of taking the vows is a recitation of the actual vows themselves and what the commitments consist of. This is recited only once, and during this section you sit normally.

If the vows are being taken from a preceptor or lama the assembly repeats the words of the vows, a few words at a time, after the lama. At the end of the third repetition of the words of commitment discussed above, the lama will say, "That is the method" (TAB YIN NO in Tibetan), and the assembly will respond, "It is excellent" (LEK SO). Then everybody performs three prostrations and sits down in normal position to repeat after the preceptor or lama the words of the specific commitments of the vows.

The other option, as was mentioned earlier, is that everyone chants together simultaneously using the liturgy. This is usually done when a lama or preceptor is not present, in which case you should consider all the buddhas and bodhisattvas to be the preceptors. This is valid because, as you will remember, you begin the recitation of the threefold repetition with the words, "All buddhas and bodhisattvas who abide throughout the ten directions, please attend me." Having in that way requested the attention of all buddhas and bodhisattvas, through their omniscient wisdom they are aware of what you are doing and therefore are proper witnesses to the undertaking of your commitment.

The eight vows can be divided into three categories. The first four vows are called the four branches of morality. The fifth vow is its own category, which is called the single branch of mindfulness or care. The last three vows are known as the three branches of discipline.

The first of these, the four branches of morality, is also called the four root vows, because they are the foundations of moral discipline. The function of the four root vows is to expel and guard against all sources of wrongdoing. This is very much like kicking out a potential thief and then locking your door securely. Therefore it is a little bit like binding yourself with a belt of discipline that protects you from wrongdoing and holds together your virtue.

These first four vows are the root of all vows in the Buddhist tradition. What distinguishes these four vows in the context of nyungne is that they are much stricter. The reason for this is that normally when someone takes the eight vows in lay *(upasaka)* or monastic ordination, they are taking them for life. In that situation the vows have to be guarded in such a way that they can realistically be kept for life. In the case of nyungne and nyinay practice, however, you are promising to keep them for only twenty-four hours. In this situation it is a very strict commitment. As you will see, this makes the benefits of the practice that much greater.

The first vow is against killing. In normal lifelong ordination this means not to kill a human being or a fetus (that which is becoming a human being). In the case of the nyungne it means not to intentionally take the life of any being, human or animal—even an insect.

The second vow is not to steal or not to take that which is not given. Whereas normally this vow means not to steal something of value, in nyungne it means anything whatsoever. For example, if you take a needle and thread from someone without permission this will break the vow in the context of the nyungne.

The third is not to engage in sexual activity, and for normal ordination this means not to engage in sexual intercourse.

Here it means not only that, but it also means not to even look upon an object of sexual attraction with desire.

The fourth one is not to lie. Normally this means not to tell lies about spiritual attainment. This entails refraining from making claims to possess spiritual qualities associated with the path that you know you do not have. However, in the context of nyungne, this vow not only means that, but it means not to lie in any way, even as a joke. This is the last of the four root vows.

The fifth vow is the single branch of mindfulness or care. This is to abstain from intoxicants, namely alcohol and so forth. The reason for this is that if you become intoxicated you become careless and mindless and the four vows will be violated. You will not even remember what the vows are, so how could you keep them? Therefore the vow is to abstain from all forms of intoxicants. This includes liquor made from grain such as wheat, drinks prepared from flower substances (like mead made from honey), and whatever is made from fruit or roots, such as wine from grapes. It refers to anything that is intoxicating.

The remaining three vows are the three branches of discipline. Their purpose is to make it easier to keep the four root vows. They involve subduing the conventional conduct of laypersons in such a way that they will have to avoid their usual activities. Avoiding the three things specified here helps you to maintain your mindfulness that you are temporarily under vows. Therefore you can enter into the excellent conduct of the victors and their children.

The sixth vow includes a vow to abstain from coquettish behavior, but it is much more specific than that. It includes two groups of three things that you have to abstain from. The first set is dancing, singing, and playing musical instruments. Dance includes any physical gesture done in order to be coquettish or graceful. It is specified that you must abstain from this whenever you take the vow unless it is prescribed by the ritual practice, so mudras may be done, but that is all. In the same way, you may not sing except for the chanting you do during the ritual, and you may not play any musical instruments except those prescribed by the ritual practice.

The second set of three things to avoid is jewelry, makeup, and perfume. This means not wearing jewelry of any kind for the purpose of ornamentation or beauty. This does not mean something like a medical bracelet which is worn only because of health needs. Finally, makeup, perfume or cologne of any kind cannot be worn on the days when you take these vows.

The seventh vow and the second of the three branches of discipline is to abstain from inappropriate nourishment, including nourishment at inappropriate times. In normal vows of ordination this means not to eat after noon, but in the context of the nyungne and nyinay it has a very particular application. On the first day of doing a nyungne you may drink all day long, but only eat once in the middle of the day. After you rise from your seat at the end of that meal you may not eat again. As for what you can have to drink all day, there is a precise description in the vinaya of the distinction between a beverage and solid food in this context. To put it simply, a beverage is something that does not require you to use your teeth. Elsewhere it is said that if you put a spoon in a substance and the spoon stands up, then it is food.

In the case of doing the practice two days in a row (a nyungne as opposed to a nyinay), on the second day you would have no food or drink whatsoever, and you keep complete silence except for chanting the liturgy and mantras. That means from the time you go to sleep on the night of the first day until you conclude the practice on the morning of the third day, you do not eat anything, drink anything, or say anything.

The eighth vow is to avoid high or fine seats or beds. "High" means any seat or bed which is higher than one cubit. A cubit is the distance from your elbow to the tip of your middle finger. This vow particularly refers to fine seats or beds such as those made with silk, tiger skin, leopard skin, or something very fine like that. The reason for this vow is to help you abstain from prideful behavior.

Those are the eight vows: the four branches of morality, the single branch of mindfulness, and the three branches of discipline. As you recite the liturgy of taking the vows, be mindful of what they are and think that you will keep these vows for the upcoming period of twenty-four hours.

After that you recite the dharani or essence mantra of the deity Amoghapasha, who is the kriya tantra form of Chenrezig. The purpose of reciting this is to protect the commitments you have just undertaken. There is an Amoghapasha mantra connected with each of the six perfections. This is the one connected with the perfection of moral discipline. By reciting this dharani you will come to possess all the moral discipline of all the buddhas of the three times. If you have previously violated moral discipline, this will purify it and you will not violate it again. This dharani is usually recited twenty-one times. It is the mantra that starts "Om Amoghashila . . ."

Next you recite the aspiration for the perfection of moral discipline. This stanza is from the section in the aspiration prayer of Maitreya dealing with the six perfections. This was an aspiration that the Bodhisattva Maitreya made three times every day and three times every night when he was on the path. It causes easy entrance into the path and speedy gathering of the accumulations. We recite that together whether or not there is a preceptor present. This is the stanza that begins, "May the discipline of morality be faultless," and so forth. If there is a preceptor present, then at this point you again perform three prostrations as a gesture of gratitude for receiving temporary ordination.

The Benefits of Observing the Vows

The benefits of moral discipline are set forth in *The Sutra that Presents Pure Moral Discipline,* which says:

> Just as someone who is unable to walk cannot walk on a road, in the same way if you do not have moral discipline you cannot traverse the path to liberation. Someone who possesses moral discipline is praised by all the vidyadharas. Someone who possesses moral discipline will achieve perfect and genuine awakening.

Further, in the *Pratimoksha Sutra* it says, "Undertaking of the four roots of moral discipline is like crossing the threshold into the palace of liberation."

In the early days of the Buddha's teaching, the benefits of keeping such moral discipline for one's whole life was, of course, tremendous—but nowadays, when we are so close to the end of the Buddha's teachings, to take these vows and keep them for even a single day is even more beneficial than it was to keep them for your whole life at the time of the Buddha. In fact, even to keep just one vow for one day at this point in history is more beneficial now than it was to keep all the various vows at the time of the Buddha. Needless to say, the benefit of taking the vows in the context of the profound yoga of deity and mantra as we do in nyungne is immense. When undertaking moral discipline in this context you join the ranks of the vidyadharas.

In the sutra called *The Illuminating Moon* it says:

> There is more merit in someone keeping the training for one day and night at this time in which the teaching of the sugatas *(buddhas)* is about to cease than there would be in venerating billions of buddhas for an innumerable amount of kalpas.

In addition, Vasubandhu said that to keep moral discipline for one day brings more merit than to engage in generosity for one hundred years. If you respect the Buddha's teachings and have confidence in their truth and validity, then you will be confident that these benefits truly do accrue.

After taking the vows you must seal them by dedicating the merit. If you do not dedicate the merit of taking the vows, then whatever merit you have accumulated can be easily lost. For example, if you become angry or jealous you can destroy this merit—and, in fact, you can destroy all the merit that you have ever accumulated. Therefore when dedicating the merit of taking the vows you include in that dedication all the merit that you have ever accumulated in the past and present and whatever merit you will accumulate in the future, and you dedicate it to great awakening just as has been done by all the buddhas and bodhisattvas of the past. Therefore, after taking the vows, the participants recite together the stanza of dedication in the liturgy which begins, "By this merit may we obtain omniscience," and so forth.

The Benefits of the Nyungne Practice Itself

In the *Tantra of the Eleven-Faced Chenrezig*, it says that by doing one nyungne you can overcome the obscurations and wrongdoing accumulated throughout forty thousand eons of continuous samsara. In particular, it explains that through the fasting of your body (which means abstention from food and drink) you purify the obscurations of body. Through fasting of speech (which means through the maintenance of silence) you purify the obscurations of speech. Through the fasting of mind (which means through immersing the mind in the meditation on the deity, mantra, and samadhi) you purify the obscurations of mind.

Not only that, but through not eating you purify the karma that would otherwise cause you to be reborn as a hungry ghost *(preta)*. Through keeping silence you purify the karma that would otherwise cause you to be reborn as an animal. Through remaining free of attachment, aversion, and apathy, you purify the karma that would otherwise cause you to be reborn in hell.

Further, through physically fasting you will come to be reborn with a good, strong physical body and an attractive appearance. Through remaining silent your words in future lives will be powerful, they will bring positive results, and whatever you say will come true. Through abandoning attachment, aversion, and apathy with your mind you will come to understand the meaning of all dharmas. This means that through fasting with the body you purify the three unvirtuous actions of body, through fasting with speech you purify the four unvirtuous actions of speech, and through fasting with the mind you purify the three unvirtuous actions of mind. In other words, through remaining free from unvirtuous action for those few days you can purify your previous unvirtuous actions.

If while doing a nyungne you become ill, this purifies the karma that would otherwise cause you to be reborn in hell provided that you still keep the nyungne vows. If you become torpid, sleepy or depressed and still continue the practice, this purifies the karma that would otherwise cause you to be reborn an animal. If you suffer from hunger and thirst, you purify the karma that would otherwise cause you to be reborn as a preta.

In *The Sutra on the Establishment of a Place* it says:

> By dipping a vase into them again and again, you could gradually empty and calculate the number of vasefulls of water in all the rivers of the world, but you could not in any way calculate the benefits of even one nyungne or nyinay.

There is great merit in offering lots of jewels and precious things to all the arhats in the world, but such merit is not even one percent of the merit of a nyungne. It is not even one thousandth of it.

In the same sutra it says, "To practice generosity for your whole life and to do one nyinay are of equal merit. To serve all arhats throughout the world and to perform one nyinay are of equal merit." Elsewhere in that same sutra it says, "If you keep the eight vows on the eighth day of the lunar month and especially during the first month, the month of miracles, then you will become awakened."

In the *Sutra of the Predictions of Maitreya* it says, "If you keep the eight vows on the eleventh day or the fifteenth . . . then you will enter my doctrine and will come to proclaim it." The meaning of this is that the karmic result of doing a nyungne on any of these days is to be reborn in the retinue of Maitreya when he appears in the world, and through this to come to attain awakening under his guidance. Many sutras and tantras have praised the benefits of the nyungne in this way.

There have been many inspiring stories about the actual immediate karmic results of doing nyungne practice. What follows is a series of short accounts of people who had accumulated extremely negative karma, but were then able to purify it by doing nyungne.

The Mahasiddha Lavapa (who was one of the 84 mahasiddhas from whom our tradition of Chakrasamvara comes) said:

> This practice of one seat and fasting or nyungne is extremely beneficial. Previously there was a man who, in order to acquire a certain woman as his wife, killed six people and their horses, but through performing this practice nine times, after his death he was reborn as a spiritual teacher. In addition, there was a hunter who performed forty-six nyungnes and after he died he was reborn in good circumstances in an affluent family. Also, there was a butcher who per-

formed eight nyungnes and he was reborn as a leader of people.

These were things that were seen directly by the Mahasiddha Lavapa. There are many other stories like this, such as the following from the Mahasiddha Nyima Baypa, or Surya Gupta. Mahasiddha Surya Gupta may be a familiar name to you if you have studied the songs in the *Ngedön Gyamtso* (*The Ocean of Definitive Meaning*) by the Ninth Karmapa, where he is quoted many times. He said:

> Once there was a very busy woman who killed a lot of animals, had one or more abortions, and seduced at least one monk, but before she died she did one hundred and eight nyungnes and was reborn as the great guru named Punyakara in southern India in the mountainous region called Shriparvata.
>
> There was a man who was doing a series of nyungne sessions and his food was stolen by a thief. Another person, a woman, brought him food to eat to continue the practice. The thief who stole the food was reborn as a preta, a kind of being that wanders all over the sky and hurts people, and it suffered tremendously. Both the woman who fed the man doing the nyungnes and the man himself were reborn as humans in affluent circumstances. There was also another woman who did twenty-five nyungnes and who was reborn as a spiritual teacher.

The Mahasiddha Mitrayogi gave the following account:

> There was a butcher who killed a lot of animals and he "kept the single seat" fifty times. After he died he was reborn as a leader of people. *(Keeping the single seat can mean either nyungne or nyinay practice, but in any case he did the practice and purified his negative karma.)* In addition, there was a particularly vicious wrongdoer who eventually started to regret how he had spent his life. By doing forty-six nyungnes he was

reborn in his next life as the child of an affluent family in pleasant circumstances.

Another story concerns the great Tibetan master Ra Lotsawa Dorje Drakpa. He was visiting a friend one day. While sitting in his friend's home he started to laugh for no apparent reason. They asked why he was laughing and he said, "This nyungne practice seems really simple but it is very powerful. I had an attendant, a woman, who previously killed five men and women and I had her do sixty nyungnes. As a result she was reborn in Shambhala with the ability to benefit beings."

Another story was told by the great master Pagmo Drupa. He said that he once had a dream that his attendant, whose name was Sonam Drak, was going to be reborn in the lower realms. He told the attendant about this, who said, "Well, why? What's wrong with me?" Pagmo Drupa said, "You are always so negative in attitude. You are ill-intentioned. That's the problem." When his attendant asked what he could do as a remedy, Pagmo Drupa gave him the transmission for nyungne. Sonam Drak did 108 nyungnes and in his next birth became a guru in a monastery in Nepal who was extremely learned and accomplished in vajrayana.

In another story, the guru Shang Rinpoche once made a remark that a certain *ngakpa* (a tantric practitioner) living in the area was a really bad fellow who liked to kill animals and lie about visions, saying that he had seen gods and spirits that he had not seen. Shang Rinpoche said, "When this person dies it is not going to be pretty. He will waste no time going to the lower states." Shang Rinpoche was a disciple of Pagmo Drupa. He was also Gampopa's nephew and an important disciple of Gampopa. Eventually what Shang Rinpoche had said made its way to the ngakpa. He was frightened, so he asked Shang Rinpoche, "What can I do about this?" Shang Rinpoche gave him the nyungne transmission and he did eight nyungnes. He was reborn in the eastern pure realm of Abhirati, the pure realm of the vajra family of Akshobhya. In that realm he became able to bring to liberation anyone with whom he had any contact.

The next story is from the Bodhisattva Togmay Rinpoche, who composed the famous text *The Thirty-Seven Practices of the Bodhisattvas*. Someone came to him and said that his parents had passed away. He did not know what kind of practice to do for their benefit and was feeling miserable. Gyalsay Togmay (as he was known) had him do the nyungne, and he did forty-eight of them. Through this, his parents obtained liberation. In addition, one of Togmay's monks was attacked by a thief, whom he killed. Regretting this and confessing it, he did the nyungne practice for five years, and both the monk and the thief obtained buddhahood.

When the Mahasiddha Karma Pakshi went to China, there was a charlatan there who gave the appearance of being a Dharma practitioner. He was teaching the Dharma but lacked any genuine qualities. He deceived people with all manner of shams and lies. Not only that, he would carelessly consume offerings made to him for the benefit of the living and the dead, neither of which he could help. Seeing this, Karma Pakshi said to him, "You have not given up the things of this world with your mind, and since you are bound by arrogance, vanity, and pride, you are going to have a very hard time in your next life." Thinking about what Karma Pakshi had said, the charlatan thought, "He is right." Stricken, he begged him, "Please embrace me with your compassion." Karma Pakshi taught him meditation, but although he practiced, he did not give rise to any experience or realization. Therefore Karma Pakshi gave him the nyungne transmission. He did one hundred of these and as a result became someone who could lead to liberation anyone with whom he had any contact.

Another story concerns a certain monk who had killed one of his friends. Regretting this, he did one hundred and three nyungnes and immediately after his death was reborn as someone who could benefit beings extensively.

There are an inexhaustible number of stories similar to these about the benefits of this practice. In addition, even if someone cannot do the practice themselves, there is great benefit to sponsoring a nyungne practice or facilitating the practice for others. This could include such things as providing the food on the first day or serving the people who are doing it.

For example, there was a woman who regularly sponsored nyungne practice sessions. When she died her body was taken to a charnel ground, and when a raven carried off some of her bones it was observed that her bones were transformed into *shariram,* which are the round pills that are associated with the bones of awakened persons.

By sponsoring a nyungne or in any way serving the nyungne participants you will accumulate tremendous merit. For example, it is said that to serve food or offer food to a nyungne participant is the same merit as offering food to an eighth-level bodhisattva. In addition, if you yourself have taken the eight vows even though you are not doing the full practice, then it is the same as offering that food to an arhat. It is said that by offering food to nyungne participants even once for one day, the result will be that in all your lives you will never suffer from famine, and for eighty or ten thousand eons you will never suffer from hunger or thirst. You will be assisted by all devas and even by asuras, yet you will be free of arrogance. Your body, speech, and mind will become free of defect and everything you wish for will occur. All obstacles will be pacified. You will be comfortable and at ease throughout all of your activities and will delight in virtue. Your longevity, merit, and prosperity will increase and you will become a disciple of all buddhas of the past, present, and future.

In short, by doing or sponsoring or assisting in a nyungne you will not be reborn in the lower realms. You will come to possess bodhicitta and will be without poverty in all future lives. Especially, you will complete the perfection of generosity. Thus, through assisting or sponsoring a nyungne you will achieve all benefits, both immediate and long term.

Therefore, if you have confidence in the validity of the Buddha's words and the authoritative commentaries upon them composed by the bodhisattvas of India and Tibet, then you should make every effort to either do the practice of nyungne yourself, assist in it, or sponsor it. In this regard, the following was said by the greatly realized master of Eastern Tibet, Vajradhara Paltrul Rinpoche:

> If you think carefully about your situation, at present it is like living on an island of cannibal demons. In that situation, make sure that you are kind to yourself, which means that you provide for your future lives. Your consciousness has wandered alone throughout the past up through the present time, driven by karma, and therefore you have been born here. However, like a hair pulled out of butter, your consciousness will be pulled out of this world when you die and you will go on alone. Seeing that fact, there is no way that you would not want to take care of your own mind. If you understand things this way, there is no way that you will not recognize the importance of benefiting yourself. If you do not do so — if you do not accomplish the divine Dharma which is the essence of benefit for yourself and others — are you not destroying yourself? Is that not true self-destructiveness? Understand this, and put it into practice.

The Benefits and Significance of Reciting the Dharanis and Mantra

Scriptural sources also describe the requirements and specific benefits of reciting the dharanis and mantra of the practice. There are three mantras used in the nyungne. There is the long dharani, the short dharani (which is the second half of the long dharani used alone), and the six-syllable mantra, *om mani peme hung*. If you do the nyungne as your principal practice and you wish to accumulate a certain number of recitations, the required number of the six-syllable mantra in the context of nyungnes is six hundred thousand. This would normally be completed in seven nyungnes. However, that does not mean that you need to stop doing it after reaching that number of repetitions.

Various sources give different mantra requirements for the dharanis. Sometimes it is said that the long dharani should be done forty thousand times and the short dharani one hundred thousand times. In that case, if you do forty thousand of the long dharani, one hundred thousand of the short dharani, and three hundred thousand of the essence mantra *om mani peme hung*, that is also considered to be a way of completing the mantra requirement of the practice.

In any case, there are certain great blessings that accrue to anyone who completes the mantra requirements of this nyungne practice of Thousand-Armed Chenrezig. It has been said that if they climb to the top of a high mountain, everyone who sees them will not be reborn in lower states. If they cross a river, everyone who drinks from that river, everyone who is struck by their shadow, everyone who is hit by a breeze that has touched their bodies, and everyone who touches them will not be reborn in lower states, and the seed of awakening will be planted in them.

In the kriya tantra it says that anyone who recites this dharani of the Thousand-Armed Chenrezig will enter into the awakening of all buddhas and the liberation of all bodhisattvas. Therefore it is called the essence of wisdom. It is also said in the kriya tantras that if you recite it even once, even the four root downfalls of a shravaka and the five actions of immediate consequence will be purified. Therefore it need not be said that it will purify any other wrongdoing. In the sutras it is said that, "If you arise early and recite this dharani (that is, the long dharani) one hundred and eight times, then you will come to possess the ten qualities in this life." These ten qualities are:

- You will be free from physical illness.
- You will be embraced by the compassion of all buddhas.
- Without effort you will have wealth and food.
- All of your enemies will be powerless to harm you and will be subdued. (This does not mean that you will actually harm them in some way. It means that the power of your compassion will cause them to relinquish their aggression.)
- You will be well-treated by monarchs and governments.
- You will not come to be poisoned, either intentionally or by natural poisons.
- You will not be harmed by epidemics or by weapons, nor will you drown. Further, you will come to possess the four qualities.[15]
- At the time of your death you will see all buddhas.
- You will not be reborn in lower states and your death will be easy.
- After your death you will be reborn in Sukhavati.

It is also said that if you recite this dharani even once in the ear of an animal who has died, it will definitely be reborn in either Sukhavati or the human realm with a good human body and a tendency toward Dharma and bodhicitta. The many wondrous aspects of all this could not be completely explained even by the vajra tongues of the buddhas. It is sufficient to say that the repetition of this dharani brings incalculable benefits.

Keep in mind, however, that all of the benefits described depend upon reciting the dharani with a one-pointed mind of devotion. You will not attain the same results if you just recite it verbally while your mind is distracted. Therefore, Vajradhara Paltrul Rinpoche said:

---

15. Apparently, the four qualities mentioned here are the remaining three points of this list of ten, with the second point counting as two, since it has two aspects.

> There is no better Dharma than the six-syllable mantra *om mani peme hung,* but no result will arise from reciting it with a distracted mouth and distracted eyes. That mind of solidification which fixates on the numbers of mantras recited should be transformed into a one-pointed mind that looks at itself as you recite the six syllables in that state.

In accordance with this, if you recite this mantra or any mantra with a distracted mind and your main concern is getting through the beads of your mala as fast as you can in order to build up the numbers, then it will not lead to the same benefit. Therefore, be mindful and alert, engaging your body, speech, and mind in the recitation, and do not be concerned with the number of mantras recited. Practice in such a way that you are constantly aware of your own mind. If you do so, then all of the benefits mentioned above will indeed arise in you, you will be able to accomplish all virtue, and you will be on the genuine path.

Paltrul Rinpoche went on:

> Look at your mind again and again. If you do so, then no matter what you do you will be on the genuine path. This is one hundred instructions condensed into one. Combining all instructions into this one point, recite the six syllables. Practice in that way.

Another part of practice for which specific benefits have been described is the prayer called *The Praise to Chenrezig.* This is part of the nyungne sadhana, and is often called the *"po praise"* because most of the lines end with the syllable "po" or "pa po." This ending in Tibetan means "the one who . . .," and each line of the prayer refers to a specific quality of Chenrezig. The benefits of reciting this are that whether you are male or female and regardless of what your particular situation may be in any other regard—if you recite this praise to the King of the Aryas (Chenrezig) with stable faith that comes from the recollection of the qualities of Chenrezig, whether you say it in the morning or evening—through reciting this praise clearly and mindfully, then in this life and throughout all future lives you will progress until you obtain the state of buddhahood. You will obtain the state that is the embodiment of the wisdom of all buddhas. Therefore in the text of the praise itself it says, "Anyone, male or female, who recites this supreme praise clearly and mindfully will, in this life or in the next, obtain the accomplishment of mundane and supermundane wishes, which is the state of buddhahood."

To summarize what we have covered so far, we can say this: the nyungne practice, including the taking of the vows, the repetition of the dharanis and mantra, meditation on the deity, reciting this praise, and so forth, is the quintessence of all Dharma. It is a practice that can be undertaken by anyone, whether they are highly receptive, somewhat receptive, or fairly unreceptive to Dharma. In any case they can still practice it successfully and through this attain all of the benefits that have been described. Therefore it was said by the bodhisattva Gyalwa Gyaltsen, "This Dharma, the Dharma of the nyungne, is a means of attainment (or sadhana) of all buddhas and all bodhisattvas rolled into one. Therefore all should practice it."

Vajradhara Paltrul Rinpoche also said:

> The single deity that embodies all buddhas is Chenrezig. The single mantra that contains the quintessence of all mantras is the six-syllable mantra. The reason for this is that when the six-syllable mantra *om mani peme hung* is explained it can be said to be, for example, the quintessence mantra of the buddhas who liberate the six realms, the quintessence mantra of the six perfections, and also the mantra that prevents rebirth in any of the six realms. Bodhicitta is the single dharma that contains all aspects of both generation and completion. The cultivation of bodhicitta contains the essence of the generation and

completion stages. Therefore, recite the six syllables within the state that knowing one liberates all.

"Knowing one liberates all" means that through understanding the main point of all Dharma, you achieve the aims of all Dharma. This is achieved through the repetition of the six-syllable mantra while understanding its benefits and significance.

Thus all of the sutras and tantras teach the tremendous benefits of this practice, which is so accessible and embodies such great blessing. Therefore, with confidence in its benefits, please embrace the practice with excellence in the beginning, middle, and end, and practice it as intensively as you can.

QUESTIONS AND ANSWERS

Question: You mentioned that the features of the palace in the visualization represent the thirty-seven factors of awakening. Could you go over those in detail?

Rinpoche: The four sides represent the first four, the four mindfulnesses. The four gates represent the four perfect abandonments. The four arches represent the four bases of miracles. The palace has five walls, which means that each wall has five layers, the way ordinary buildings have plaster and then sheetrock and so on, these walls have five layers of five different kinds of jewels. These represent the five powers and five strengths. The seven factors of awakening are represented by the garlands of jewels that are strung around the upper part of the walls, just below the roof of the palace, and the roof is supported on the inside by eight pillars. Those eight pillars represent the noble eightfold path.

To give more detail, the four objects of mindfulness are: body, sensation, mind, and dharmas. The fourfold perfect abandonments are: (1) abandoning all wrongdoing that you are doing; (2) not undertaking further wrongdoing; (3) cultivating all virtue that has not yet been cultivated; and (4) continuing to practice all the virtue that you are practicing. Then there are the four miraculous bases (often translated as the four miraculous legs or wheels). These are: motivation, diligence, mindfulness, and one-pointedness.

The five strengths are the strength of karmic seed, the strength of momentum, the strength of renunciation, the strength of familiarization, and the strength of aspiration. These are described in the *lojong*[16] teaching in the *Great Path of Awakening*.[17] The five powers are the same in name as the strengths. The strengths arise first, and as they develop and become more intense they become powers.

The seven factors of awakening are: (1) perfect memory; (2) seeing all phenomena as they are; (3) diligence in benefiting beings; (4) perfect joy in working for beings; (5) blissfulness, peacefulness, and clarity of mind and body; (6) samadhi; and (7) perfect equanimity.

The noble eightfold path consists of perfect view, perfect thought, perfect speech, perfect action, perfect means of sustenance, perfect effort, perfect mindfulness, and perfect samadhi.

Question: Having been brought up in the United States, I have the sense that I have been living in one of the most materialistic societies that has ever existed. Since I have grown up in that environment, it is not always easy for me to see my attitudes clearly, since I am caught up in the mindset of my upbringing. I am talking about the attitude that having money and possessions is extremely important, and that other things are not so important. Do you have any suggestions as to how I can see those attitudes and remedy them?

---

16. Lojong is a Tibetan word that literally means "mind training."
17. This is one of the most important mahayana texts of Tibetan Buddhism, which describes the mind training of a bodhisattva.

Rinpoche: The only solution seems to be to practice contentment. If you lack contentment, no matter how much stuff or how much money you have you will never be happy because you will always want more. There is no limit to what you can want. There is no amount that you cannot exceed in your imagination, so therefore no matter how much you have, if you lack contentment you will never be happy with it. If you have a hundred dollars you will want a thousand. If you have a thousand you will want a million. If you have a million you will want a billion. If you succeed in owning an entire country, then you will want a second one, and so on. That is why wars happen. There is no way that the amount of acquisition itself can ever complete the process of acquisition. Therefore Nagarjuna said, "Wanting more defeats one's aim like a poisonous fruit, whereas contentment is the greatest wealth because it alone brings satisfaction."

Question: I have a question about the mantra repetition. As I understand it, mantras are vibrational. Is it best to say them deliberately and bring that vibration into your being in a distinct way? Often in practice the mantra seems to go very fast and there is a tendency to lose all the distinction of the vibration and it pretty much becomes a blur, so to speak. Is that as beneficial as saying it slowly and getting all the vibrations, or do you want to be saying it rapidly and having just the one vibration?

Rinpoche: Well, everyone tends to chant mantras at their own speed. It should not be so fast that the sounds are indistinct and it should not be so slow that it is ponderous. There is nothing wrong theoretically with chanting the mantra slowly except that you want to say as many of them as possible. At the same time if you go too fast and the sound is slurred, that is not good either, so you need to find a happy medium.

Bardor Tulku Rinpoche

Nevertheless, some people can chant mantras much faster than others. It depends on the agility of your tongue. Some people can say a mantra very quickly and keep the pronunciation distinct, but others are not able to go that fast.

REST FOR THE FORTUNATE

The Title, Subtitle, and Invocation

What we have covered so far has been a general look at the practice of nyungne. Now we will study nyungne in much greater detail by going through a complete traditional Tibetan text on the subject. This present book, in fact, takes its title from that traditional text, *Rest for the Fortunate,* which was composed by The Ninth Situ Rinpoche, Pema Nyinje Wangpo (1774-1853). It was preserved in a collection of works by Jamgön Lodrö Thaye, who is also known as Jamgön Kongtrül the Great. The word "rest" in the title means a respite from the sufferings of samsara and from the accumulation of the causes of that suffering. The term "fortunate" refers to those who have the good fortune to do this practice of nyungne and therefore will derive its benefit. Some of the subject matter will review what we covered in the Introduction, but for the sake of keeping the teaching on this text intact, it will be taught more or less in its entirety here.

The subtitle of the text is *A Brief Explanation of the Benefits of the Fasting Practice of Renewal and Purification Consisting of Eight Branches in Connection with the Sadhana of the Thousand-Armed Chenrezig.* The reference to eight branches in the subtitle refers to the eight vows that are taken for a period of twenty-four hours. If they are taken for one period of twenty-four hours, that is called abiding for a day, or nyinay. In the practice of fasting, or nyungne, they are taken on two consecutive days. The specific vows and the benefits of taking them are also discussed in detail. The term "renewal" in the subtitle refers to the fact that these eight vows are taken in the context of the mahayana practice of the renewal of moral commitments and bodhicitta. "Purification" refers to the power that this practice has for the purification of wrongdoing. Finally, the subtitle indicates that all this is done in the special context of the practice (sadhana) of the Thousand-Armed Chenrezig (Avalokiteshvara).

The initial section of the text is in verse. As is traditional, this has two parts: the initial invocation, and the statement of the author's intention. The invocation, which is an homage, has three sections. The first section is a one-line Sanskrit homage, *Namo Guru Lokeshvara*, which means "homage (or salutation) to the guru inseparable from the Bodhisattva Avalokiteshvara (Chenrezig)."

The second section of the homage is a four-line stanza of homage to Chenrezig. It says, "You embody in one all of the bodies and realms of the innumerable victors and their children." Because Chenrezig embodies the compassion of all buddhas and bodhisattvas and because compassion is the essence of their awakening, he embodies in one single form all of the qualities of all buddhas and bodhisattvas including their realms, their bodies, and their wisdom.

The text continues:

> Therefore, embodying all of those in one, with your immeasurable wisdom of compassion, with the immeasurable wisdom which is the display and result of compassion, you empty samsara from its depths for as long as space exists.

For as long as space will continue to exist, Chenrezig will continue to empty samsara from its depths. This means he will reach down with his compassion and his wisdom into the very depths of samsara and bring suffering beings to a state of liberation. "For as long as space exists" means forever. Chenrezig has promised never to abide in the nirvana of buddhahood until all sentient beings without exception have been liberated through his efforts alone into a state of perfect awakening. Therefore his generation of bodhicitta and his resultant state of compassion are superior to those of others. For that reason, the first stanza of invocation ends with, "You who hold a lotus in your hand, protect me until awakening." The term "holder of the lotus" is a synonym for the Bodhisattva Avalokiteshvara. He is usually shown holding a lotus flower in one of his hands. Here, the writer asks that Chenrezig protect him until he himself attains awakening.

The third section of the invocation is addressed to the gurus of the lineage of this practice. It says, "For the benefit of beings in the age of degeneration, you, the Lord of the World, display appropriate forms to tame each being individually." "The age of degeneration" refers to the times we live in. "The Lord of the World" (or Lokeshvara in Sanskrit) is a synonym for Bodhisattva Avalokiteshvara, or Chenrezig. Because we do not have the good fortune to perceive Chenrezig directly, he takes birth in the form of incarnations in order to reach us.

Then the author mentions some of those who are incarnations of Chenrezig in that way. The first one he mentions is Bhikshuni Lakshminkara, who originated this practice of nyungne. She was a bhikshuni (nun) and her name was Lakshmi or Palmo. Also mentioned are the Tibetan King Songtsen Gampo and the Gyalwa Karmapa. All of these beings are emanations of the Bodhisattva Chenrezig.

Then he supplicates, "Root and lineage gurus, please abide on the stamens of my heart." "The stamens of my heart" uses the metaphor of the heart as a lotus flower. Thus it means, "Please abide in the midst of my heart until I attain awakening." That completes the invocation.

The second part of the text is the statement of intention. It begins, "That great ship of Dharma which liberates beings from the sufferings of the ocean of existence..." The meaning of this is that what the author is going to explain is like a great ship of Dharma which can bring beings across the ocean of existence and suffering. It continues, ". . . is the profound quintessence of the sutras and tantras difficult to find even one time out of a hundred." The expression "one time out of a hundred" refers to a certain flower which is very rare and only blooms once every one hundred years. Here it refers to the fact that it is difficult or rare to be born human, and even more so to have a precious human existence. Even more so, it is rare to encounter the Dharma, and even more so to encounter these teachings, which are the quintessence of all Dharma. All the teachings of the sutras and the tantras are condensed into this one practice.

He continues, "Mere contact with this closes the door to lower states." Any contact with this practice, such as doing the nyungne even once, sponsoring it, and so forth, forever closes the door to rebirth in lower realms of existence. He concludes the stanza with the words, "I will briefly explain the benefits of abiding in the fast." "Abiding in the fast" is the literal meaning of the Tibetan term *nyungne*.

PART ONE

Introduction

Next is the main body of the text, which is in prose. It says:

> Here, I am going to briefly explain the benefits of the practice of Arya Avalokiteshvara in connection with the fasting done in the context of the mahayana renewal and purification. This practice has three aspects. First is the mahayana practice of renewal and purification. Second is fasting. The physical aspect fasting means (if it is done as a two-day practice) eating only certain foods and only once on the first day, and on the second day abstaining from all food and drink. The verbal aspect of fasting means keeping silence on the second day. In this practice, the fasting, the mahayana motivation, and the third aspect, the sadhana of Chenrezig, are all brought together, making it especially profound.

The main text has three parts. The first is a general statement of benefits, the second is a detailed explanation of benefits, and the third is an "important digression" on further implications of the practice.

The first part has four sections. The first three sections are concerned with keeping the eight vows in the context of the hinayana, mahayana, and vajrayana respectively, and the fourth is concerned with the benefits of keeping one seat.

Taking and Keeping the Vows According to the Hinayana

This first section has three topics. These are: (1) how the vows are maintained; (2) the shortcomings of not maintaining them; and (3) the benefits of maintaining them.

The first topic involves several questions. The first is: Who takes them and keeps them? The answer is that these vows are suitable to be taken by any man or woman who is a householder, which is to say someone who is not a monastic. Strictly speaking, a monastic, having taken lifelong vows, does not need to take the temporary vows since they would be redundant. (As you will see later, however, in the mahayana context these vows are appropriate for monastics as well.)

The second question is: How are they taken and kept? The answer is that those who wish to take the vows should do so in the presence of someone who possesses the lineage of the vows. At best this means a fully ordained monastic or bhikshu, or it can be a novice monastic or an upasaka (layperson) who holds these vows. When taking the vows you first renew the vow of refuge, because the foundation of all upasaka or lay disciple ordinations including this day-long ordination is the vow of refuge. It is called "the vow of an upasaka who holds the three refuges." Thus the first part of any ordination ceremony is the renewal of going for refuge to the Buddha, Dharma, and Sangha.

Following that, the eight specific vows you take are repeated after the preceptor three times, and at the end of that third repetition you automatically receive the vows. Then from that time onward until the vows expire you keep them. The vows are taken before dawn on the day on which they are to be kept. Because the time of dawn changes, they are usually simply taken before 5 AM. They expire automatically at dawn or sunrise the next day because they are twenty-four-hour vows. Therefore if you do the complete practice for two days, you retake the vows each morning. Regardless of how long you continue doing the practice, the vows automatically expire at sunrise on the day after they are taken and must be retaken again every day. In addition, each time they are taken, they must be taken from a preceptor. If you are going to take the vows many times there are some additional procedures for how that is done, but these can be learned elsewhere.

Furthermore, when you take the vows you need to do so with the proper motivation. Taking the vows in order to be protected from immediate danger such as governmental or legal prosecution or for some sort of magical protection against sickness or spirits is not considered to be an appropriate motivation. It is also considered inappropriate to take the vows for the purpose of obtaining your own relative benefit, such as the hope that by taking these vows you can be reborn as a god or as a human. The motivation that is prescribed by this tradition is to take the vows out of full renunciation for all of samsaric existence. Therefore you should take the vows in order to transcend not only the lower states but finally all of samsara.

Taking the vows in that way, you maintain them through the faculties of mindfulness (or recollection) and alertness. Mindfulness means remembering what the vows are, and the faculty of alertness means being observant in guarding against any action that transgresses the vows.

The next question is: When are these vows taken and maintained? Traditionally there are particular times of the year and month when it is considered most auspicious to take the vows. There are four lunar months within the year, such as the month of miracles and so forth, when it is customary for communities or individuals to take these vows and do the associated practices. In addition, within each month there are particular days when it is traditional to do so, such as the eighth day of the waxing moon, the full moon day, the new moon day, and so on. We will go into detail about these auspicious days and months in a later section.

However, it is a mistake to think that it is best to wait until some kind of auspicious or special day to do the practice. As soon as you generate the attitude of wishing to do the practice and you have the necessary conditions, the place to do it, and so forth, then go right ahead and do it. This is an important point because the duration of a human life is uncertain and the worst obstacle to Dharma is procrastination. Sometimes we use the pretext of waiting for an auspicious occasion as an excuse to procrastinate. The most important thing is that you actually *do* the practice. Don't worry too much about *when* you do it.

The final part of this topic concerns the details of the vows that are taken. Since we covered this earlier in the book we will not do so again here. However, in addition to these eight vows, Lord Atisha added two more that have become traditional, and which we abide by when we do the practice. The first is to eat only vegetarian food during the practice, and the other is to take purification water whenever re-entering the room where the nyungne is taking place.

The Shortcomings of Not Keeping the Vows According to the Hinayana

Next we will consider the shortcomings of not taking or not keeping these vows. First of all, however, you need to recognize what is wrong with doing negative actions in general, whether or not you have a vow.

By taking life you cause yourself to be reborn in the three lower realms. If you intentionally take the life of another being out of anger or hatred you will be reborn in hell, if you do so out of desire you will be reborn as a preta, and if you do so out of apathy you will be reborn as an animal. Most often, if you take life you will tend to be reborn in hell and most particularly in what is called the reviving hell among the eight hot hells. Even if you should succeed in being reborn a human being after taking life, your life as a human will be very short. You will be ugly and you will be unintelligent. You will be paranoid, constantly afraid, and usually angry; you will be plagued by chronic illness, be miserable, and will always feel that you lack whatever would make you happy. For every time you intentionally take the life of another being, depending upon the particular circumstances, your life will be taken at least three hundred times in future lives and up to as many as a thousand times for each life, depending upon the particular circumstances of each act of killing.

Through stealing you will be reborn in the wailing hell, which is again one of the eight hot hells. Even when you are born as a human being you will be utterly impoverished, and unable to acquire any kind of resources, prosperity, or affluence. You will not only be born impoverished, but you will remain impoverished for the duration of that life. What little you have will be lost to you. You will be disliked and persecuted by others without apparent reason.

The karmic results of improper sexual activity is that you will be reborn in the great wailing hell, which is worse than the last one. Even if you are reborn as a human, for five hundred consecutive lifetimes you will be reborn as a leper or as someone with incomplete faculties, either mentally or physically. You will be reborn as someone of unfortunate appearance or as a hermaphrodite. You will constantly be afflicted by life-threatening circumstances and will have many enemies.

Through lying you will be reborn in the black line hell, which is a hot hell where you are marked by something like a chalk line and then cut up with burning saws. When you are born human you will be unable to speak. You will be without compassion, and you will be jealous and competitive. You will smell bad, and throughout all your lifetimes you will be unable to understand spirituality.

Through drinking alcohol you will be reborn in a particular type of hot hell where molten iron is forcibly and continually poured down your throat. Even if you are born as a human being, you will be sleepy, dull-minded, and forgetful. Your mind will never be clear. You will be paranoid and fearful. You will be without a personal or social conscience, jealous, greedy, and without any virtuous qualities whatsoever. You will be reborn five hundred times as a harmful spirit or as a dog or as an insane person.

These are the results of performing those five types of actions individually. Any of them will produce rebirth in lower states for many lifetimes and bring about the suffering resulting from such births. Therefore, they are called inherently negative actions. Whether or not you have taken vows not to engage in them, doing these things always leads to these consequences. If you have taken vows not to do them, then the results are a hundred thousand times worse — that is, more intense and longer in duration.

The Benefits of Keeping the Vows According to the Hinayana

Next we turn to the third topic, which is a description of the benefits of taking the vows and the benefits of abandoning the actions which would violate those vows.

The general result of abandoning unvirtuous deeds such as the four root actions described above as well as refraining from the consumption of intoxicants, is that you will achieve rebirth as a human or god. In addition, by abandoning each one of these actions, you will experience a result that is the opposite of what performing the action would have led to. For example, just as killing will lead to short life and sickness, abstention from killing will lead to long life free from sickness. Abstaining from each of the actions in a general way has its own particular benefit, and each act of abstention has its own particular benefit that corresponds to the action itself.

When these negative actions are avoided in conjunction with the twenty-four-hour vows, the benefits are even greater. This was taught by the Buddha in the *Sutra Requested by Nechog*. Nechog begins by addressing the Buddha and saying, "Suppose there were two people, one who devoted his or her whole life to the practice of generosity, and the other who once, for one day, observed the eight vows for one period of twenty-four hours. Which of these two would accumulate the greater merit?" In response the Buddha said:

> Nechog, the merit of someone keeping these eight vows for one day and the merit of someone who devoted their whole life to the practice of generosity are in no way equal. Imagine if someone filled the entire world including all its regions—the sixty regions of India and so on—with precious materials such as diamonds and sapphires, and with great exertion offered this to all the holy beings such as arhats and bodhisattvas and others that there are in the world and also offered robes to the religious, medicine to the ill, and other acts of generosity. The amount of merit that that person would accumulate by engaging in such tremendous generosity with such diligence for their whole life is not even one hundredth or one thousandth the amount of merit that would be accumulated by the second person who merely keeps these eight vows for one day. Nechog, therefore abide in these eight vows. Especially take them in the waxing phase of the month of miracles. In that way you will enjoy all the splendor of gods and humans.

The following was written by Vasubandhu:

> If someone out of great faith were to practice generosity intensively for one hundred years and someone else were to keep perfect morality for one day,

the merit of that second person would far exceed that of the first. If you had to you could eventually measure the amount of water in all of the five great main rivers of India, such as the Ganges and so on. You could measure them jar after jar. It would take a long time but you could do it. But you could never measure the merit accumulated by one day's observance of the eightfold moral discipline. By doing this once, for one day, you ensure rebirth in the first god realm, the realm of the four great kings; by doing it twice you ensure rebirth in the second, the realm of the thirty-three. By doing it three times, you ensure rebirth in the third, the realm beyond dispute. Doing it four times ensures rebirth in the fourth, the joyous; five times, in the fifth, delight in emanation; and six times will bring rebirth in the highest of the god realms of the desire realm, mastery over the emanations of others.

In other sutras it says that by doing this even once you will be reborn as Indra. In the *Bodhisattva Pitaka* and in many other sutras, it says that by doing this even once you will never be reborn in lower states in all your future lives. Whenever a buddha appears in the world you will encounter him. Your morality will always be pure, whatever aspirations you make will be accomplished, and through making a connection with the Three Jewels in that way, through making offerings, going for refuge, and so on, you will, in the future when Buddha Maitreya appears, be born in the innermost circle of his retinue. About this, *The Sutra of Prophesy of Maitreya* says:

> Those who venerate the Buddha Shakyamuni by presenting parasols, victory banners, perfumed garlands and ointment, and so on will definitely have their place in my retinue. Those who make offerings of saffron water and sandalwood-scented ointment and make these offerings to Buddha Shakyamuni will have their place in my retinue. Those who continually venerate the Buddha and take refuge in the

Sangha and engage in virtuous actions will have their place in my retinue. Those who have properly undertaken moral discipline during the teachings of Buddha Shakyamuni and have maintained that in accordance with their commitment will definitely take their place in my retinue. Those who have presented Dharma robes to the sangha, as well as food, drink, medicine, and so forth will definitely take their place in my retinue. Those who every half month or on the fourteenth day or the fifteenth (which means on the full moon day, or on the eighth day, or for the first two weeks of the month of miracles, and so on), in short all of those who perform the renewal and purification through the eight vows will definitely take their place in my retinue.

By implication we can also infer from Maitreya's statement that by taking and keeping these vows for twenty-four hours and dedicating the merit of this to the aspiration to be reborn in a pure realm such as Sukhavati, a person can achieve rebirth in whichever pure realm they wish.

The Benefits of Keeping the Vows for One Day

In the previous topics we described the benefits of keeping the eight vows in general. Next we will discuss the benefits of simply keeping these vows for twenty-four hours in and of themselves, whether or not they are kept in the context of a nyungne practice.

It was stated in the sutras that if on the eighth, fourteenth, fifteenth, and thirtieth days of the lunar month you keep these eight vows, then you will become "just like me." This was actually said three times in three different places by three different people. It was said by Buddha Shakyamuni, it was said by the Arhat Shariputra, and it was said by the Deva Indra. Therefore it can be inferred from this that by keeping these eight vows for twenty-four-hour periods you will attain all of the qualities of Indra, of Shariputra (i.e., of an arhat), and of a buddha.

In another sutra it says:

> Abandoning the taking of life, you will attain the vajra body. *[This means the indestructible body of a buddha, which is beyond birth and death.]* In the same way, by abandoning stealing and so forth — in short, by abandoning the seven unvirtuous actions of body and speech — you will acquire all the qualities of a buddha such as the particular shape of a buddha's fingers and toes, the golden wheel imprint on the soles of the feet and palms of the hands, the complete faculties, and great strength.

This refers to the actual shape of the Buddha's features, his tongue, the sound of his voice, and his teeth. The Buddha had forty teeth, all very even and white, the saliva that improves the taste of all food, and the physical scent of moral discipline. In short, all of the qualities, the marks, and the signs of physical perfection on the body of a buddha are produced by this practice of moral discipline. By paying homage to those worthy of veneration, one acquires the crown protuberance of which no one ever sees the top. In other words, no matter how tall you are, if you try to look at the top of a buddha's head it is always a little bit above you. That is a result of a Buddha having paid homage to worthy beings in previous lives.

Those are obviously the long-term results, but in terms of the immediate results, in the sutras it says if you keep these eight vows for even one day you will be liberated from the age of warfare. If you offer one pill of *arura* (an herbal medicine) to a monastic you will be liberated from the age of epidemic illness. If you offer one bowl or one measure of food you will be liberated from the age of famine.

Then there are other benefits. For example, the benefit of abandoning eating after noon is that wherever you are born in all your future lives there will be good harvests and there will be no problem with getting enough to eat and drink. By abandoning ornamentation such as garlands and jewelry, and coquettish behavior such as dancing and singing, you will always have a pleasant appearance with a good physical smell and your faculties will be clear. By abandoning sitting on a great or high seat you will always be respected and praised by others. You will have no problem getting bedding and horses to ride and so on. There are innumerable benefits of this sort.

All the benefits described up to this point are those of simply keeping these eight vows according to the pratimoksha, which means according to the discipline of the hinayana or common vehicle. These benefits accrue even if keeping them is not motivated by bodhicitta and when they are not taken in connection with the vajrayana practice of nyungne.

Taking and Keeping the Vows According to the Mahayana

Next the text discusses the even greater benefits that accrue from taking the vows of the nyungne practice under certain very special conditions. The first condition is when they are taken in the context of the moral discipline of the mahayana. This means that the actual vows are not merely vows of individual liberation. In the mahayana, the intention of each vow is to avoid wrongdoing as part of the moral discipline of the bodhisattva vow. Therefore it has even greater benefits than those mentioned in the previous section in connection with the hinayana or common vehicle. The second condition is when they are taken in the context of the renewal and purification practice taught in the lower tantras.

First we will consider the great significance of these vows in the context of the mahayana, which is the way we actually do it in our own tradition. This has three topics: how the vows are to be kept, the defects of not keeping them, and the benefits of keeping them. Keep in mind that what was presented before was about the benefits if they are taken as individual liberation vows. What follows is going to be much stricter.

In the hinayana context, it was mentioned that only lay people can take the vows because monastics already have lifelong vows. However, the vows may be taken by both lay and monastic practitioners when taken in the context of the mahayana practice of renewal and purification, because in that case they are a branch of the bodhisattva vow. They are relevant and beneficial to monastics because the mahayana vows involve temporarily undertaking a much stricter version of the commitments that monastics already have. This will be explained in detail as we continue discussing the vows.

You will remember that at the beginning of the present text it said you can receive these vows from any upasaka, shramanera, or bhikshu. However, if you are taking them in the mahayana form as we do, they cannot be taken from just any monastic. They must be taken from someone who possesses the lineage of the mahayana vows of renewal and purification. In addition, the words of the ordination are different. You say, "For the benefit of all beings" and so on, as you will find in the nyungne liturgy. When you take them in this way you are taking them with the motivation of bodhicitta, and they therefore become a part of the bodhisattva vow. Because of this, you only need to receive these vows from a preceptor the first time you take them.

This is explained as follows: when discussing the eight vows as hinayana vows, it was said that you must retake them from a preceptor every day because they expire after a day, and when they expire you no longer possess them. In the mahayana, however, you are taking them with the motivation of bodhicitta, which means that even though the vow expires after twenty-four hours, the seed of the vow, which is bodhicitta, is still there. Therefore, although you are not governed by the strictness of the vow, you still possess it.

That is why after taking it once from a qualified preceptor, you can retake it at any time you wish during your life.

You will find this point clearly explained in the longer nyungne liturgy texts. In general, the bodhisattva vow involves three types of discipline. These are the disciplines of (1) abstention from wrongdoing; (2) engaging in the benefit of others; and (3) the accumulation of virtue. Here you are intensifying the first of these. Therefore although the vow expires, you do not lose it, because the mode of its generation is bodhicitta.

One obvious difference between taking these vows in the mahayana context and the pratimoksha vows is that the pratimoksha vows are normally taken for a whole lifetime, whereas these vows expire after twenty-four hours. However, that is not always true. In *Ratnakuta's Sutra* and other places, it says that if you wish you can take the pratimoksha vows for a lifetime or for any period of time you wish. Someone who takes the vows in this way is called a "gomen upasaka," a name derived from the great master Chandragomen, who took them in this way.

When you take them in the context of the mahayana, the actual vows are the same as in the hinayana. However, because they are taken for a shorter period of time, because they are an intensification of the moral discipline of the bodhisattva vow, and because the bodhisattva vow is more concerned with the avoidance of the three unvirtuous actions of mind than it is with the seven unvirtuous actions of body and speech, the vows are much stricter. That is why you will find additional restrictions that were not mentioned in connection with the vows of individual liberation.

We will use the first of the vows, the vow not to take life, as an example. In the pratimoksha vow, whenever you take a vow not to kill as an upasaka or as a monastic, you take the vow not to intentionally kill a human being or human fetus. In the mahayana context, however, when you take the vow not to kill for twenty-four hours you must also not kill any kind of animal or insect—anything, no matter how small. This applies not just to beings you can see, but even to beings you might unintentionally step on. To keep the vow, you have to try to avoid doing that. Because the vow in this context is part of the bodhisattva vow, it would be a violation of that commitment to mentally abandon those sentient beings by not protecting them from harm. Here, therefore, the twenty-four-hour vow not to kill is extremely strict. On the other hand, in the pratimoksha form of the vows you only fully break the vow if you intentionally kill a human being or fetus, and if you kill an animal it is only a violation. In the mahayana there is no distinction between a violation and a break. The vow is completely gone if you intentionally or through negligence kill any being whatsoever. In addition, you not only have to be concerned with what is explicitly forbidden, but with everything that is similar, including states of mind.

In that way all of the eight vows are much stricter in the mahayana form. For example, with regard to eating, in general according to the pratimoksha you can eat any time from dawn until lunchtime, but in the mahayana practice of nyungne or nyinay you can only eat once, and as soon as you get up from that meal you have to stop eating for the day. In addition, there are further restrictions about what you can eat. In the pratimoksha there is not as much concern with what you are eating as there is with when you are eating it. In the mahayana context, what you eat becomes especially important. You cannot have any bit of meat or blood in your food during those twenty-four hours. Concerning liquids, you can have any drink as long as it is really liquid. You can have milk, tea, water and so on at any time during the day, and it is permitted to have sugar or honey in your drinks.

What follows next in the text is an explanation of why eating meat is in direct contravention of the Buddha's commands and the mahayana. First we have a quote from the Buddha:

In the sutras called *The Garden of the Cattle*, *The Great Cloud*, *The Ratnamegha Sutra*, *The Sutra of Nirvana*, *The Angulimala Sutra*, and *The Lankavatara Sutra*, I clearly forbade the consumption of meat.

This was stated by the Buddha because he knew that in the future people were going to say that it was permitted to eat meat. In those sutras the defects of the sin of eating meat were clearly stated. In a text by Manjushri called *A Brief Summary of the View* it says the following:

> Killing animals in order to acquire the substances of their body and buying with money what has already been killed for the purpose of eating it are equally killing. Those who engage in either one of these at any time will burn in the hot hells such as the wailing hell. Those who say Manjushri says that there is no sin in a householder buying the meat of an animal that has already been killed should consider why there would be merit in buying a statue that has already been cast. If you can accumulate merit by buying it and setting it up on a shrine, then you can certainly accumulate demerit by buying the meat of an animal that has been killed.
>
> Those who kill animals out of desire for wealth will burn in the hells for a hundred thousand eons. Those who buy and eat the meat out of attachment for it will burn in the hells for ten million eons. Any person who eats meat will first of all be reborn as a preta, and after that will be reborn in the hot hell known as the wailing.

In this way, Manjushri summarizes the statements made by the Buddha in those previously mentioned sutras. It is also said that whenever meat is eaten, the smell of the cooked meat causes subtle beings that are almost invisible to us to faint almost to the point of death and the smell terrifies the spirits. In addition, since all beings have been your mother countless times, any time you eat the flesh of any being, you are eating your mother's body. The text continues:

> The consumption of meat by Buddhists is a cause for others to lose faith in the Buddha's teaching and to denigrate it. For those who eat it, it is a cause of being reborn as flesh-eating demons, wolves, and so on. At the end of many such rebirths they will fall into far worse states. In brief, these sutras say that anyone who eats meat is not a follower of the Buddha, and the Buddha himself said, "I am not the teacher of those who eat meat."

Additionally, since it seems that onions and garlic have similar defects, then they are also to be avoided when doing nyungne or nyinay in the context of the mahayana practice of renewal and purification.

This section concludes with the remark, "This was just an incidental aside."

All of these quotations about meat in particular are from the mahayana sutras, and one will find different statements made about these matters in various scriptures, in other sutras, and in the tantras.

To comment on this,[18] we would have to say that once you are born in this world, you have to eat. If you analyze the situation, you will see that there is actually no kind of food that you can eat that does not bring with it some kind of obscuration because there is no way to eat without in some way bringing harm to others. Therefore as an ordinary person you cannot realistically hope to avoid all acts of wrongdoing.

In the case of bodhisattvas, some bodhisattvas will eat meat because it can benefit the beings from whom the meat came.

---

18. Bardor Tulku Rinpoche added the following comments to the statements made in the text.

If you are born as a human being, you have many opportunities to make contact with bodhisattvas by social interaction, by making offerings, and so forth. Animals do not have that opportunity. If, however, the body of an animal that has already been killed is eaten by a bodhisattva, that being forms a connection which will be beneficial to it in the future.

The Shortcomings of Not Keeping the Vows According to the Mahayana

The next topic concerns the shortcomings of not keeping the vows. This is very brief because most of it is the same as what was mentioned in the earlier section on the shortcomings of not keeping the vows in the context of hinayana. However, what needs to be added here are the shortcomings if one does not generate bodhicitta, because the essence of the eight vows in the mahayana context is the generation of bodhicitta. In short, as is taught in all of the mahayana sutras, if you do not generate bodhicitta, then there is simply no way to attain buddhahood or full awakening. In this regard, Lord Gampopa summarized the situation as follows:

> Someone who does not generate bodhicitta and therefore will not engage in the excellent deeds of a bodhisattva is simply not practicing the mahayana. Without practicing the mahayana there is no way that they will ever attain perfect awakening.

Bardor Tulku Rinpoche

The Benefits of Keeping the Vows According to the Mahayana

Through the generation of bodhicitta as your motivation for doing the practice, your wrongdoing will be quickly purified. That means that even though keeping the eight vows in general is a tremendously powerful force for the purification of previous wrongdoing, when the motivation for it is the mahayana motivation of bodhicitta, it becomes even more powerful. Through doing this you will also perfect the accumulation of merit and you will gain the ability to benefit not only yourself but others as well. This means that through generating bodhicitta in connection with the nyinay or nyungne practice, you establish the infallible cause for your quick attainment of buddhahood.

In *The Sutra Requested by Paljin* it says:

> If the merit of one instant's generation of bodhicitta had physical form it would be larger than all of space. In the *Bodhicharyavatara* it says, "All other virtues are like water trees, they yield their fruit once and then die. However, the virtue of bodhicitta is like a tree that yields perennial fruit. As it yields fruit, it continues to grow and flourish." Therefore, even the worst wrongdoing is destroyed in an instant by the superior force of bodhicitta, just as the universe is destroyed by a fire at the end of an eon.

Taking and Keeping the Vows According to the Vajrayana

Now we come to an explanation of how the vows are kept, the defects of not keeping them, and the benefits of keeping them according to the vajrayana practice of the nyungne itself; that is to say, the integrated practice of the fasting ritual motivated by bodhicitta and accompanied by the meditation practice of the Eleven-Faced Chenrezig sadhana.

First of all, anyone who does the practice is — at least while doing the practice — a practitioner of the kriya and charya tantras which are the original scriptural basis for this practice. Therefore anyone who has received an empowerment for any of the major kriya or charya deities of any of the buddha families, and especially of the padma family, is also authorized to do the nyungne practice. Nevertheless, this practice is not limited just to those who are already intensively involved in the practice of kriya or charya tantra. Because the particular deity that this practice focuses on is the Bodhisattva Chenrezig, who is the presiding deity of this tradition of Buddhism, then it is the intention of the holders of this lineage that this practice be made available to anyone who wishes to do it. That could mean someone who knows nothing more about it than how to chant the mantra *om mani peme hung* all the way to someone who is involved in the highest yoga tantra practices. This practice is considered to be appropriate for and available to everyone. If someone who has very little practical background does it, then they will get a great deal out of it. If someone who has a great deal of training and knowledge does it, they will get a great deal out of it as well.

In general, whenever you do a practice like the nyungne, it is best if you have received the permission blessing, which is the type of empowerment that authorizes the practice of the nyungne and imparts the mantra and the reading transmission for the text. Often all of these things are given together. That authorizes you to meditate on this deity and recite these mantras. However, even if someone has not received the specific empowerment and reading transmission for the practice, if they have received an empowerment for the principal deity of one of the three wisdom families of kriya tantra, such as Mitrukpa of the buddha family or Amoghapasha of the padma family and so on, then having entered into one of those mandalas they are authorized to do all the practices of that particular buddha family.

Nowadays, however, the tradition has become quite flexible as to how the nyungne practice can be introduced to people. One way this is often done is that before the nyungne begins, after the vows are given on the first morning, the transmission of the dharanis (the long mantras) is given by their being recited three times by the preceptor and repeated thereafter by the participants. That can serve as a preliminary empowerment if it is not possible to get the formal empowerment first. When it is done that way, then at the conclusion of the nyungne the participants may be given the full empowerment (which in this case is the permission blessing of that deity) so that they can thereafter continue to do the practice, or do it again later. In short, at best one should receive the empowerment for the nyungne before doing it. If this is not possible, it is still permitted to do the nyungne provided you receive the vows at the beginning of the nyungne and the transmission of the mantras.

In this section we are concerned with the full practice, which is a kriya tantra practice and therefore has certain requirements above and beyond the eight vows. This is a practice that integrates all three vehicles, so it includes the motivation of bodhicitta and the meditation of kriya tantra in addition to the eight vows. Therefore you have the additional requirements of kriya tantra to observe. For example, on the second day, which is called the main day of the nyungne, you cannot eat or drink anything, and this discipline is kept strictly such that you cannot put so much as a grain of food or a single drop of water into your mouth. In addition, according to the tantras themselves you have to be extremely careful about what would normally be regarded as ordinary physical occurrences such as yawning and flatulence. These must be guarded against at all costs. If you do either of these things then, strictly speaking, you need to be ritually purified by the preceptor again with the water from the vase.

At best, when doing a nyungne practice the mind should be one-pointedly focused on the generation and completion stages of the practice.[19] If that is not possible, then at least do not allow your mind to be overpowered by random thoughts. Even if you cannot rest your mind one-pointedly on the visualizations and so forth, then at the very least it is important to perform the practice, the liturgy recitation, the mantra repetitions, and so forth with an attitude of faith, enthusiasm, and compassion. In short, always maintain a virtuous state of mind.

On the main day of the nyungne, you do not speak. Nowadays we interpret this to mean abstaining from ordinary speech and conversation of any kind. There are two ways this can be interpreted, however, depending on your level of accomplishment. Those practitioners who have a fully developed practice of the generation and completion stages should abide in what is called "verbal fasting," which means abstinence from making any kind of sound whatsoever—worldly or spiritual—with their speech. When someone practices in that way they do not even chant the liturgy out loud; it is all chanted mentally. They would also abstain from physical movements such as prostrations and circumambulation, and focus their body, speech, and mind one-pointedly on the deity and mantra.

---

19. In simplest terms, the generation stage refers to the visualization of the deity and the meditation and rituals that go with that, whereas the completion stage refers to resting in the natural state of mind at the end of the generation stage. Sarah Harding has done an excellent translation of Jamgön Kongtrül Lodrö Thaye's text on this subject entitled *Creation and Completion* (Wisdom Publications).

Most people who do the nyungne practice do not have a stable practice of the generation and completion stages, however, so it would be pointless for them to do it that way. They would be not only refraining from unvirtuous speech, but from virtuous speech as well. In effect, then, they would just be sitting there in a state of neutrality. Therefore, the way the nyungne is done these days is that on the main day you abstain from all mundane conversation, but in order to accumulate virtue you recite the liturgy melodically out loud and recite the mantras audibly. In addition, you are physically active by engaging in virtuous actions of body such as prostrations, circumambulation, and so forth.

Ordained practitioners must wear the three robes of a monastic while doing the nyungne. Others should wear clean clothes that do not contain fur or leather products. During the days of the nyungne practice, you must engage in a ritual ablution called an "ablution of the five limbs" three times. This is done first when you get up, and then it has to be repeated twice more during the day. The mala or rosary that you use can be strung on cotton thread or synthetic, but not leather.

In short, the practice consists of engaging in physical austerity through fasting, prostrations, and so forth. As well, there is the verbal austerity of silence, and the mental state of one-pointed virtue where you do not allow your mind to be sullied or disturbed by mundane thoughts. In that way you try to develop and maintain a state of the utmost purity of body, speech, and mind throughout the practice.

The Shortcomings of Not Keeping the Vajrayana Vows and Ritual Requirements

The second topic in this section concerns the defects of not keeping the vows and the other ritual requirements of the nyungne. The basic point of this is that you really cannot do a practice of the kriya or charya tantra without observing the vows and commitments such as the fasting practice, the vegetarianism, and so forth. The reason for this is that in all aspects of vajrayana the specific type of conduct must always accord with the specific type of practice. The view, meditation, and conduct always go together. If you attempt to do a vajrayana practice without maintaining the rules of conduct required by that specific practice, then you are not keeping the samaya or commitments of the practice. If you have no samaya there is no basis for your practice. The root of the practice has rotted away and there is nothing left. You will not succeed in getting any kind of results. In fact, even beyond that, the practice will become counterproductive and will actually lead you in the opposite direction from its intended purpose.

In general, the things that you abstain from in the nyungne practice are also things that are problematic anyway. Eating a lot, drinking a lot, and talking a lot all cause many thoughts, and thoughts cause kleshas which prevent us from experiencing samadhi (meditative absorption). Therefore, by simply placing your body, speech, and mind in the austerity of the nyungne practice, most of the bad habits of body, speech, and mind are at least temporarily put in abeyance. This is called the fasting of body, fasting of speech, and fasting of mind. This makes it much more effective when you do the meditation practice associated with the nyungne.

Bardor Tulku Rinpoche

The Benefits of Keeping the Vows According to the Vajrayana

The third topic in this section discusses the benefits of doing the full practice of the nyungne. The briefest way to summarize these would be to say that they are the opposite of the defects that were just mentioned. There is a great description of the benefits of nyungne found in the text called the *Collection of the Intentions of All Tantras*. It says:

> If a son or daughter of good family *[which means a practitioner of the mahayana]* does a nyungne once, simply by doing that they purify all the wrongdoing that they have accumulated throughout forty thousand eons. They will certainly achieve rebirth as either a human or a deva. If someone does the nyungne eight times *[this refers to the custom of doing the practice of the two-day nyungne eight times sequentially]*, one after the other, they will attain the same state as that of a stream enterer. *[A stream enterer in the common vehicle is the first of the four levels of spiritual attainment.]* They will certainly be reborn in the realm of Sukhavati. If they perform twenty-five nyungnes they will become equal to a once-returner. *[A once-returner is someone who attains a second level of attainment according to the common vehicle.]* They will purify all of their wrongdoing for the previous eighty thousand eons. If someone does fifty nyungnes they will attain the state equivalent to a non-returner *[the third level of attainment according to the common vehicle]*. Because this is done in the context of the mahayana and vajrayana, it is superior to the common vehicle's attainment. In addition, they will purify their previous wrongdoing for eight hundred million previous eons. If someone does one hundred eight nyungnes one after another they will attain the equivalent of arhatship *[the fourth and highest level of attainment according to the common vehicle]*. They will purify all of the wrongdoing

and obscurations that they have accumulated over one billion eons. They will definitely be reborn in the realm of Sukhavati in the direct presence of the buddha Amitayus.

Those are all general benefits of the practice. Then there are specific benefits, which correspond to particular aspects of the practice. Because you are engaging in physical austerity through fasting, prostrations and so forth, you purify your previous physical wrongdoing, including the taking of life, stealing, and sexual misconduct. Because you are abstaining from food and drink, you purify the karma that would otherwise cause you to be reborn as a preta. You also pacify sickness and other disturbances. You will cause yourself to have a majestic presence and fine appearance in future lives, and ultimately this physical fasting is the cause of the attainment of the marks and signs of physical perfection when you attain buddhahood.

Because you are fasting verbally, which means keeping silence, you purify the wrongdoing of speech such as lying, slander, harsh speech, and meaningless babbling. You will not be reborn as an animal, and in future lives you will have great power of speech. You will naturally tend to speak honestly and straightforwardly — and never meaninglessly. Ultimately you will attain buddhahood and you will have the sixty limbs of melody which distinguish the speech of a buddha from that of any other being.

Because of the fasting of mind, which means abstaining from ordinary mundane thoughts and directing your mind one-pointedly to meditative absorption while doing the nyungne, you purify mental wrongdoing such as covetousness, spitefulness, and wrong view. You will not be reborn in a hell realm. You will give rise to meditation experience and realization. In future lives your awareness will be clear and sharp, and you will always be able to understand the meaning of Dharma. Ultimately, when you attain buddhahood and give rise to the five wisdoms, the full wisdom of buddhahood, this is a result of the fasting of mind.

In addition, the specific unpleasant experiences and deprivations you undergo when you do a nyungne take the place of what would otherwise be much worse karmic consequences of previous actions, and therefore the nyungne purifies those actions. For example, when you do a nyungne and you get very hot from doing the prostrations, or you get very cold because of various conditions where you are doing it, or you feel physically sick because of the fasting, and so on, this purifies the causes of rebirth in hell.

The intentional and willing experience of hunger through fasting and of fatigue through practice will prevent your rebirth as a preta. By resisting the tendency to fall asleep which is produced by fasting, by resisting the tendency to just space out and let your mind become obscure, and by using your energy to focus your mind on the practice, you purify what would otherwise cause rebirth as an animal. Thus every aspect of the practice has its own specific and tremendous benefits.

Instructions and Benefits of Keeping One Seat

Now we turn to the fourth section, which is concerned with what is known as "keeping to one seat." This practice comes from the monastic tradition of the common vehicle. In its most general sense, "one seat" literally means doing your practice in one place for the whole time you do it, especially during a retreat. You do not move your seat around in the shrine room, for example, or move to another location. That is the basic idea of "one seat."

In the context of the nyungne and nyinay practices, "one seat" has also come to have another specific meaning which refers to the custom of eating only once on a practice day. You eat at midday in one sitting. Once you get up from your seat, you cannot eat any more that day. This is done on the first of the two days of a nyungne and also on any day that you do nyinay, the twenty-four-hour form of the practice.

Rest for the Fortunate

The custom of eating only once is variously known as "one seat," "one fire," or "one water."

The benefits of this are tremendous, and it is something that in and of itself is extremely simple and easy to do. Anyone can do it, whether they are someone with the highest faculties and involved in the most elaborate form of vajrayana practice, or beginners doing the most simple kind of practice. It is within everyone's reach. It is simply a matter of taking the vows and restricting yourself to that one meal, and this can be done for one day or for a longer period if you wish.

If it is the first time you are doing it, you must take the eight vows that morning from someone who possesses the lineage of these vows and, as described above, on that day you only eat once. In addition, you can have whatever beverages are appropriate under the vows at any time during the day until you go to sleep. If it is the first day of a two-day nyungne, then you have one meal and beverages throughout the first day, and nothing to drink on the second day.

The traditional dividing line between what constitutes a beverage and what constitutes solid food is this: If you put a spoon in it, does the spoon stand up or not? If the spoon stands up, it is considered solid food and can only be consumed during the midday meal.

Traditionally, whenever you do this practice — either on the first day of the nyungne or in the more simple context of just taking the vows and eating only once that day — there are certain procedures that accompany the midday meal. Before the meal, the sutra called *The Noble Recollection of the Three Jewels* is usually chanted, and sometimes a select portion of the food to be consumed is reserved and placed as an offering on the shrine. Also, before the conclusion of the meal all those eating make a torma offering in which they make the impression of their five fingers. This is called a "handle torma" or *changbu*. They make the impression of their fingers in some of the food—in the bread or rice or something like that—and it is presented to the hungry ghost called Hariti.

In any case, the midday meal is consumed without rising. If you need more food than you have initially taken, there have to be people around who have not taken the vows to serve it, because those who have taken the vows cannot eat another thing that day once they stand up.

Auspicious Months and Days to Do the Practice

As we discuss the times when it is most auspicious to do this practice, please keep in mind that it is *always* virtuous to do this practice, so do not think that you should only do it at special times. In addition, even when you cannot do the full practice of the nyungne on the auspicious days of the month and year, you will still attain the benefits associated with these occasions if you are able to observe the discipline of the eight vows, including the single meal.

First we will discuss dates that are auspicious to do the practice according to the yearly calendar. The Buddha performed a sequence of miracles during the first two weeks of the first month of the Asian year. Therefore, that first month is called the "month of miracles," and keeping the discipline of one seat for the first two weeks of that month is considered a very powerful act of virtue.

The fourth month of the Asian year is the month during which the Buddha was born, then thirty-five or thirty-six years later attained awakening, and forty-five years after that passed into parinirvana—all in the same month. Thus it is the month that commemorates his awakening and also his birth and death. Usually it is said that he was born on the eighth day of the fourth month, and that he attained full awakening and also passed away on the fifteenth day, the full moon day. Some say that he passed away on the eighth day of that month. That is less commonly agreed upon, but certainly he was born on the eighth and attained enlightenment on the fifteenth day. Therefore, the fourth month is considered to be the coming together of these three different auspicious occasions in the Buddha's life, and this entire month and these specific days in particular are a highly auspicious and beneficial time to do the practice.

The sixth month of the Asian year is called the "dharmachakra month" because on the fourth day of that month the Buddha first "turned the wheel of Dharma," which is a traditional way of saying that he presented his spiritual teachings.

Finally, during the ninth month of the Asian calendar, the Buddha descended from the heaven of the thirty-three Vedic gods where he had spent the summer teaching his mother, who had been reborn there among the devas. For that reason, the whole ninth month is considered sacred. Specifically, on the fifteenth day of the ninth month he promised to return to Earth, and then on the twenty-second day he actually descended from that heavenly realm and returned to Earth.

Thus the four great occasions are: (1) the first half of the month of miracles (the month beginning with *Losar*, Tibetan New Year); (2) the entire fourth month, especially the eighth and fifteenth days; (3) the fourth day of the sixth month (the first turning of the wheel of Dharma, which is known as *Chökor Duchen* in Tibetan); and (4) the twenty-second day of the ninth month (the descent from heaven or *Lhabab Duchen* in Tibetan). This set of four great occasions is what are most commonly observed, and you will usually find these on practice calendars.

However, some people use a set of eight great occasions throughout the year. In that case, added to the above are the following four dates: (1) from the eighth day until the fifteenth day of the twelfth month of the Asian calendar, which is the occasion of the Buddha's sitting in front of the

Bodhi tree; (2) from the first day until the eighth day of the second month, which is the occasion of the Buddha's conception; (3) the fifteenth day of the third month, which is the occasion on which the Buddha taught the Kalachakra, his ultimate teaching, at the Drepung stupa in southern India; and (4) the eighth day of the tenth month, which is when the Buddha's parinirvana is commemorated by some traditions (according to some accounts he did not pass away in the fourth month but at this time).

On all these dates whatever you do is considered to be very powerful. Any virtuous or unvirtuous action is believed to be at least one hundred thousand times more powerful for good or evil than it would be normally.

Now we come to auspicious days according to the monthly calendar. What follows is a description of the benefits not only of keeping the one-meal discipline (nyinay) on these various days, but also combining that with the supplication of particular buddhas on these particular days.

On the first day of every lunar month it is taught that the deva known as Kumara comes to Earth to examine the moral quality of human behavior. If on that day you recite the *Samadhiraja Sutra* or supplicate the Buddha in the context of that sutra, and especially if you recite the vow of refuge and any mantra and keep the discipline of eating one meal, you will purify the wrongdoing you have accumulated throughout forty eons. You will also free yourself from possible rebirth in the hell of swords and spears, where beings are cut up and pierced by such weapons.

On the eighth day of any lunar month, the deva known as Dechen comes to earth to examine the longevity of humans. If you supplicate or recite the name of the Medicine Buddha and recite his mantra, you will purify thirty eons worth of wrongdoing. You will be freed from the hell of mutilation, where beings experience being cut up into little pieces.

On the fourteenth day of the lunar month, the representative of Yama called Wangpo Jajin comes to earth to record the moral quality of human actions. If you recite the names of the thousand buddhas of this fortunate eon and pay homage to them, you will purify the wrongdoing of a thousand eons and you will be freed from the hell of boiling water.

On the fifteenth day, Brahma comes to earth to examine the moral quality of human actions. If you recite the name of the Buddha Amitabha and his mantra, you will purify the wrongdoing of two hundred eons and you will not be reborn in the cold hells.

On the eighteenth day, Yama Dharmaraja himself comes to examine the moral quality of human actions. If you recite the name and the mantra of Chenrezig, you will purify the wrongdoing of ninety eons and be free from the hell of the pit of swords, where beings slide down a hill and get pierced by countless swords.

On the twenty-third day of the lunar month, the deva Maheshvara comes to earth to examine our morality. If on that day you supplicate the Buddha Vairochana, you will purify the wrongdoing of a thousand eons and will not be reborn as a preta.

On the twenty-fourth day of the month, the representative of Yama, Wangpo Techen, comes to earth. If you recite the name and mantra of the bodhisattva Sai Nyingpo, this will purify the wrongdoing of a thousand eons and will also liberate you from rebirth in the hell where beings get cut up into little pieces.

On the twenty-eighth day of the lunar month, Indra, the ruler of the devas of the thirty-three-fold heaven, comes to earth. If you recite the name of the Buddha Amitabha on that day you will purify ninety eons of wrongdoing and will be liberated from the black line hell. This refers to something like a chalk line which snaps on your body, and you are cut on those lines.

On the twenty-ninth day, the ten protectors (or guardians of the ten directions) come to earth. If you recite the name of the Medicine Buddha at that time, you will purify the wrongdoing of a thousand eons and will be liberated from the hell of burning ashes and burning sands.

On the thirtieth day, which is the new moon day in the Tibetan calendar, the god Brahma comes to earth. If you recite the name of Buddha Shakyamuni and his mantra then, you can purify the wrongdoing of a thousand eons and be freed from rebirth in the hell where beings get crushed to fragments.

In general, the benefits of hearing the name of any one of these buddhas or bodhisattvas and of reciting the six-syllable mantra *om mani peme hung* even once on any of these days cannot be explained even by the buddhas and bodhisattvas of the ten directions. It is said that the benefit of keeping the discipline of one seat even once is incalculable, and even if done only once in your entire life will free you throughout all future lives from famine. For ten thousand future eons you will have an abundance of food and drink. You will be protected and assisted by devas and spirits. You will be free from all defects, and you will have longevity, affluence, and good reputation in future lives. Finally, as a result of your motivation, you will come to achieve the great non-abiding nirvana.

Therefore the practice of eating once a day in the context of taking the eight vows is extraordinarily beneficial. What follows are several short examples of these benefits for people who had accumulated various kinds of negative karma.

There was a butcher (this means someone who slaughters the animals, not just cuts them up after they are already dead) who took these vows and ate only once a day fifty times. Rather than being reborn in lower states, he took birth as a ruler who was very virtuous. There was a woman who had managed to kill six people through stealth; she performed this discipline of keeping one meal thirty-nine times, and she was reborn as a human being who was virtuous and practiced Dharma. Another woman did this discipline of eating once twenty-five times and was reborn as a great Dharma teacher. There are a lot of similar accounts of the benefit of doing this. However, if you have confidence in Dharma, then what I have just said is enough for you to extrapolate the rest.

To do the practice of a deity other than the Thousand-Armed Chenrezig on an auspicious day, you get up early and wash and put on clean clothes. Then take the eight vows for that day. In Nagarjuna's *Friendly Letter*, it says the Buddha taught that there are six things to be recollected: the Buddha, Dharma, Sangha, generosity, moral discipline, and the devas. Therefore, in preparation for the practice, occupy your mind with recollection of these six things.

To do this, after arising and taking the vows, you first recite the refuge vow, the generation of bodhicitta, and then some form of the Seven-Branch Prayer. Then, in the sky in front of you, you visualize the particular deity that you wish to practice that day. You should also visualize the Bodhisattva Chenrezig because he is the presiding deity of this tradition as a whole.

In the writings of the Tibetan King Songtsen Gampo, he says to visualize Chenrezig in his four-armed form on the left of whichever deity you will be practicing that day. Then you recite the names of the deities, pay homage to them, and go for refuge to them, repeating this liturgy a hundred or a thousand times—as many repetitions as you have time for. Then you recite the individual mantras of the particular deity for that day and the six-syllable mantra *om mani peme hung* as many times as you can. Teachings and texts are available elsewhere to learn the practices of these various buddhas, including the names that are to be recited, the mantras, and so forth.

Next imagine that from the forehead, throat, and heart of each of the deities rays of light emerge that strike you and all sentient beings, purifying all wrongdoing and obscurations of body, speech, and mind. Then, imagine the entire environment and all sentient beings melting into light and dissolving into the deities in front of you. After that, you imagine that the deities dissolve into emptiness, and you rest without conceptualization. Finally, dedicate the merit.

You can do this practice four or six times in the day if you wish, eating only one meal around noontime. Though it is best if you can do the whole practice of nyungne or nyinay, if you cannot and you practice in the simple way just described, it will still be extremely beneficial for you.

The source for the associations of certain days with certain buddhas and bodhisattvas comes originally from the sutras and is based on the particular activity of those buddhas and bodhisattvas. The practice of eating only once a day and taking the eight vows is found in both the common vehicle and in the mahayana. The actual style of practice described here comes from the writings of King Songtsen Gampo, who is considered an emanation of Chenrezig.

This first part of the text ends with a note of criticism. The author says that in today's world our relationship to the unsurpassable, profound, and secret meaning of the teachings of both sutra and tantra is merely imaginary. We do not really practice them properly, despite the fact that we have all the necessary conditions and freedom to do so. If under these circumstances we do not so much as grab onto the end of the path, then we are just fooling ourselves. Therefore, it would be good if people at the very least would make some kind of connection with a Dharma practice such as this, which is so easy to do, has no dangers, and is of such great benefit. The author concludes by saying, "That is what I think, and I just mentioned it as an aside."

Rest for the Fortunate

Some Personal Advice

I would like to give you a larger context for the material that we have just gone through. When you hear explanations such as these about the benefits of Dharma practice, it may sound as if doing any of the practices just once is enough, and at that point you would have "got it made." However, though the explanations of the benefits that this text and texts like this provide are 100% accurate, the effectiveness of the practice depends upon the degree of your own faith and diligence. The compassion and blessings of buddhas and bodhisattvas is all-encompassing and impartial. It is like the light of the sun. Buddhas and bodhisattvas do not think, "This person is my devotee, so I must help him. That person is an adherent of a different religion, so I am not going to help him." It is your faith and diligence that determine the degree to which you are receptive and can therefore receive the blessings and benefits of the buddhas, the bodhisattvas, and the Dharma.

Because the compassion and blessing of buddhas and bodhisattvas are not conceptual, not partial, and utterly all-encompassing, they are therefore immeasurable. They embody what are traditionally called the four immeasurables: immeasurable love, compassion, joy, and impartiality. Wherever there is space there are sentient beings, and all sentient beings are filled with karma and kleshas. It is the commitment and purpose of all buddhas and bodhisattvas to establish all of these beings ultimately in buddhahood, and temporarily in a state of comfort, freedom from sickness, and so on.

It is true that if you have great faith and great diligence, then even just practicing for one day will bring all the benefits that this text has described. It is important to remember that this depends on what you yourself bring to the practice. Keep in mind the remarks written by the author at the conclusion of this section. He is saying that we are often too lazy to do the practices, or even when we somehow get around to doing them we have so much doubt about the benefits that the doubt itself interferes with whatever practice we do. In other words, either we do not do it at all or we do it halfheartedly. If you want practice to be effective it needs to be diligent on the one hand and also free of hope and fear — namely hope for certain results and fear that it will not work.

The second thing I would like to mention is that through the aspirations of His Holiness the Karmapa, and through the aspiration of countless buddhas and bodhisattvas, there are now many centers of the Karma Kagyu tradition throughout the United States and around the world. It is very important to listen to Dharma teachings carefully, and to do your best to scrutinize their meaning and come to a definitive understanding. Through hearing the teachings and contemplating their meaning, you can resolve doubts and misunderstandings.

Nevertheless, while those activities are important, hearing the teachings and thinking about them is not sufficient and will not bring about the intended result. Thinking about the meaning of the teachings will reveal their meaning to you in a personal way. However, what is most important is to actually experience that meaning. For this, you have to practice meditation. The power and benefit of nyungne practice is so great that, even if you were not able to have the time or opportunity to do much other practice, even just doing the nyungne practice once a year will be of great benefit to you.

One day, each and every one of us is going to die. Even if we were extremely wealthy or ruled the whole world, and no matter what we accumulated or how much power we possessed, we would not be able to take so much as one needle or one spool of thread with us when we die. Likewise, even if we were the poorest person in the world and only owned one empty clay bowl, we would not be able to take that bowl with us when we died. It is essential at the very least to be able to achieve a state of confidence and freedom from regret in our minds such that we can say to ourselves at the time of death, "I have done this; I have practiced this much; I have had a meaningful life." You can achieve this by doing the practice of nyungne.

The practice of nyungne holds special significance for those of us who follow the tradition of the Gyalwa Karmapa, who is considered to be the embodiment of the blessings and activity of the buddhas of the past, present, and future, and the embodiment and incarnation of Chenrezig. As well, we have to consider the connection between this bodhisattva and all buddhas. In a praise of this specific form of Chenrezig it is said, "Your thousand hands are the thousand Chakravartins and your thousand eyes are the thousand buddhas of this eon."

Since His Holiness embodies Chenrezig and all buddhas, including all buddhas of this eon as well as Chenrezig, the practice of this deity is especially important for us. If we analyze it, in fact, we could say that this entire tradition has arisen through the activity and the direct intervention of the Bodhisattva Chenrezig.

In addition, and not surprisingly, the practice that became most widespread in Tibet as a practice for laypeople is this very nyungne practice. This is significant because, though they were very widespread in India, most practices of kriya tantra did not take root very well in Tibet. As we have discussed, kriya tantra depends upon being very clean. You have to wash a lot, and Tibetans simply do not like to wash! However, the one kriya tantra practice that the Tibetans really did manage to do was the practice of the nyungne. This is true in part because they combined its kriya tantra aspects with the anuttarayoga meditation practices. By doing so, they reduced the amount of washing that was actually necessary down to the ablution of the five limbs, which eventually turned into just scattering a few drops of water on the face, hands, and legs, and leaving it at that.

In any case, I think that this practice can and will flourish in this culture. We have seen evidence of this. When we first started doing nyungne retreats, there would be five or six people. Now it is not uncommon to have as many as fifty people participate. Also, a lot of the practice consists of fasting. This is something that everyone in this country seems to be very interested in. Because you have no trouble in acquiring sufficient food, you are more concerned with eating less than with eating more!

QUESTIONS AND ANSWERS

Question: I understand that the food is vegetarian but also excludes onions and garlic. Why is that?

Rinpoche: There are a lot of things said about the different reasons for these particular rules, but the simplest explanation is that they tend to make you sleepy.

Question: I am taking medication. What should I do during nyungne?

Rinpoche: If there is a medical requirement to receive medication then the traditional way is that the person would inform the presiding lama and then take the medication as usual. In general you could say that there is a slight defect in doing this, since you are ingesting something and perhaps taking some water to swallow pills. But practically speaking, what you should do is just make sure that the presiding lama knows about it and then do it.

We need to make a distinction between the presentation of Dharma and the actual application of it while we are still in samsara. Dharma has to present the full story, including the final results and implications of actions. Therefore when a virtuous action is mentioned, all of the good things it can or will lead to will be mentioned. When negative action is described, all of the outcomes it can lead to must be mentioned as well. However, when you are actually applying these teachings in your life, you simply have to do your best. You do what you can in terms of engaging in virtue and avoiding wrongdoing. In addition, if you aspire to go beyond what you can presently do with the intention of being able to do more in the future, then I think that is sufficient.

Question: If you have a medical condition like diabetes and you are on insulin medication and you really cannot fast, is there any part of this practice that can still be done?

Rinpoche: In all medical situations, exceptions can be made on an individual basis by the presiding lama. You should inform the lama leading the practice of your medical need, and he or she can give you permission or acknowledge your need to make an exception. There are two approaches that are usually taken in this kind of case depending upon the actual medical needs of the individual in question. If someone really needs to be able to drink liquids and to eat at least something during the day, then he or she can take the same vows and do the same practice, but instead of doing a nyungne where the second day is a complete fast, they could simply do two consecutive nyinays. Both days would be treated like the first day of the nyungne. That is the solution if it is required that the person eat solid food. The other situation is if solid food is not required but medication must be taken, which requires that a small amount of liquid be taken with the medication. In that case, you could do the nyungne and otherwise avoid all liquid and nourishment on the second day, just taking the minimum of water needed to take the medicine.

Question: Are the rules for keeping the lay vows and the pratimoksha vows the same?

Rinpoche: Because the lay (upasaka) and pratimoksha vows are taken for a lifetime, they are not as strict as those taken during the nyungne practice. The basic definition of what violates lay vows is in accordance with the pratimoksha tradition. That is the case even though you may take it in the broader context of the mahayana. For example, in terms of the vow not to kill, in the lay vows you are promising not to kill a human being or human fetus.

To break a pratimoksha vow such as the upasaka vow, four elements have to be present, otherwise the vow is not broken. There has to be: (1) intention; (2) the basis, which is the actual object in relation to which the vow is broken; (3) the implementation of the intention (in other words, you not only wish to achieve something but you also have to do something to achieve it); and there must be (4) the completion of the act, i.e., the fulfillment of that intention. Unless these four are all present the vow is not broken.

The nyungne vows are much stricter and easier to break, since they are taken in the context of a short and intensive meditation retreat.

Question: As I understand it, the first time we participate in a nyungne it has to be given by a preceptor. Who can it be led by after that, in subsequent times that we do it? Also, is the confession before the Thirty-Five Buddhas a practice that people can do on their own, as a separate prayer?

Rinpoche: In answer to your first question, from the point of view of an individual, the first time in your life you do a nyungne you have to receive the nyungne vows from a preceptor. Having done that once, you can thereafter do the practice at any time on your own if you wish to, in which case you would take the vows in the presence of the Buddha, Dharma, and Sangha. In the case of groups (because there will always be one or more people in that group who have not done a nyungne), there should always be a lama present to serve as a preceptor. Lamas can perform their duties in one of two ways. If they wish, they can actually ordain the people, which means he or she would recite the vows and the participants would repeat the vows after them. It is also acceptable for the lama and the other participants to chant the vows together simultaneously. It can be done either way, and how it is done is up to the presiding lama.

Rest for the Fortunate

In answer to your second question, the confession of downfalls which is usually called the *Thirty-Five Buddhas* is considered the single most effective confession liturgy in our tradition. Therefore it is not only permitted, but it is very much recommended that you recite it as often as you can.

Question: I connect in a very straightforward way with the teaching of the Four Noble Truths, but when the various hells and those sorts of things are mentioned it is a lot harder to relate to.

Rinpoche: It actually does not matter a great deal whether you pay that much attention to the detailed descriptions of the various hell realms. The descriptions of these sorts of things by the Buddha were made in order to inspire renunciation for cyclic existence so as to encourage us to enter the path that leads out of cyclic existence, and to illustrate the results of actions. If you get the basic point about cyclic existence, then whether or not you take specific illustrations to heart is less important.

Question: When the hell realms are spoken of we are used to thinking of them as being in a certain place, but according to Buddhism wouldn't it be more like a state of being, such that it is not in some particular location?

Rinpoche: It is actually presented both ways in the Buddhist tradition, which brings up the topic of what are called "indicative" and "definitive" statements by the Buddha, and the general notion of indicative and definitive meaning. In certain contexts in the teachings of the common vehicle and specifically in the common abhidharma, it is stated that the hot hells and the cold hells have definite locations or distances under the ground and are located in particular places and so on, as you mentioned in the first part of your question. In the higher abhidharma characteristic of the mahayana and in the teachings of the mahayana in general, it is taught that the experience of hell is a projection of a mind that is imprinted by wrongdoing. Therefore it could not be a physically existing place because it would be impossible to create or maintain such an environment. The way we understand it in our tradition is that the first description of hell, where it is said to have a specific location, is an indicative statement, which means that it is one that requires further interpretation. The second interpretation, that hell is a projection of the mind afflicted by wrongdoing, is seen as a definitive statement, i.e., one that does not require further interpretation.

Question: This question is about deities. As I understand it, they were once actual people, but when we speak of the deities in terms of their actual essence, they are somehow internal or inherent within ourselves. Could you explain that further?

Rinpoche: The answer to this question is similar to the last one in the sense that both interpretations are true depending on whether you look at it from the point of view of indicative or definitive meaning. Let's use Chenrezig as an example. In terms of his true nature, Chenrezig is the compassion of all buddhas embodied in the form that we visualize. It is not understood that there is literally a being out there somewhere who has four arms and so on. Instead, this form is the way we meditate upon Chenrezig in order to encounter the qualities that he represents. In that case, we are concerned with the essential nature of Chenrezig. However, it would be too simplistic to leave it at that and deny that he is "out there." He is also "out there" because he has emanations or incarnations such as His Holiness the Dalai Lama and His Holiness the Gyalwa Karmapa. When you meet either of them, you are meeting a person who is distinct from yourself but who is also an embodiment of Chenrezig.

Even beyond that, if you practice meditation assiduously, for example the meditation on Chenrezig, then eventually you might actually have a vision where you encounter the deity face to face. Thus it is both inside and outside. There are many, many accounts of people meeting deities such as Chenrezig face to face. For example, the origin of the nyungne lineage was a vision in which the Bhikshuni Lakshmi saw Chenrezig face to face and received this transmission from him. In the same way, many individuals in India and many other countries have had visions of this and other deities.

Question: I imagine there are many people who have friends or family members who have aborted fetuses. I would like to know if in our practice of the nyungne it is possible in some way to dedicate our merit to help reverse this negative karma for them.

Rinpoche: Yes. You can do that, and it will help.

Question: What is the Buddhist position on birth control?

Rinpoche: As far as we know, birth control did not exist at the time of the Buddha and so he made no statements about it. Thus he neither recommended nor forbade birth control. It is up to each individual to make up their minds. If you want my opinion, I think it is obviously a far better thing than abortion. The practice of birth control tends to reduce abortion and so therefore I think it is to be encouraged.

Question: Could you discuss the Buddhist point of view concerning the sexual relationship between married people, the vows involved with that, and perhaps sexuality in general?

Rinpoche: Well, there are three separate issues here, and because this text is dealing with two of them the whole thing can get a little bit muddled. To make it clear, the three issues are: the issue of the morality of sex in general, the issue of adultery, and the issue of sexual acts by someone who is bound by a vow not to engage in them. These are three distinct issues. The first point, which is the really bad news, is that from the Buddhist tradition's point of view, sexual activity is inherently unvirtuous or negative. It is negative because the Buddhist understanding of cyclic existence is addiction and attachment, and sexuality is one of our strongest attachments and addictions. The problem with it is not that someone is necessarily being hurt. What is wrong with it is that it reinforces the attachment which brings about and maintains cyclic existence. That is why, even under the best circumstances, it is still considered somewhat negative. However, the degree to which it is unvirtuous varies dramatically, depending on the situation. The unvirtuous dimension of sexual activity in a committed relationship, for example, is tiny compared to the situation of adultery or if there is a violation of the vow of celibacy.

In the case of someone who has no vows governing their sexual behavior, sexual activity will still have a negative impact on them by reinforcing their attachment. It is similar to the way a child who is too young to know that fire burns will still get burned even though they do not know that fact. However, this is entirely different from the situation in which someone has a vow either to abstain from adultery (which is the lifelong vow of a layperson), or to abstain from sexual activity for twenty-four hours during the nyungne practice. If you take the vow not to commit adultery and thereafter you have sex with someone who is not your spouse, that is extremely unvirtuous far beyond the generic negativity of sexuality. In the same way, if you take the twenty-four-hour vow of celibacy and you break it by having sex, that is extremely negative. Those two negativities are much greater than, and to some extent separate topics from, the basic issue of sexuality itself which is based on the problem of attachment.

Question: In regard to the basic issue of attachment in relation to sexuality, is it correct to say that the ideal situation according to Buddhism would be for us to completely give up any attachment, whether it be to loved ones or to possessions?

Rinpoche: Ordinary situations like sexual activity are considered negative in the context of what is known as "the pervasiveness of suffering." The Buddhist view of life in general is that it consists of three different types of suffering. One is called "the suffering which is suffering." This is the experience of mental or physical pain of any kind. That is what we would normally regard as suffering, especially when it is compounded, meaning that one problem is occurring on top of another.

The second type of suffering is called "the suffering of change." This has to do with changes that occur over time and involve the impermanence of a previous experience of well-being.

The third one is much harder to recognize than the other two, and is the real context for understanding the negativity of sexuality. This is "the pervasiveness of suffering." In essence this simply means that even though you may not be suffering right now, what you are doing is probably accumulating the causes of suffering in the future, but you do not recognize it. It is a little bit like walking around and thinking everything is fine, but meanwhile there is an underground lava flow that you are unaware of that is just about to burst through the ground and burn you up. We do not recognize the presence of the lava below the ground, whereas an awakened person would see that it is there. We are insensitive to the pervasiveness of suffering and we do not feel that suffering is there until it actually hits us. The traditional example for this is that if you put a hair in the palm of your hand you probably would not even know it was there, and it certainly would not bother you. But then if you took the same hair and put it in your eye it would bother you tremendously. Ordinary beings, which means most of us, are like the palms of the hand. We are too insensitive to be aware of the suffering around us. An awakened person, on the other hand, is like the eye. They are sensitive to — and really feel — the suffering that is inherent in all situations.

Question: I am wondering about the relationship between the benefits and the possible negative results of taking vows. I assume there would be positive results from keeping the vows properly, but if something happens and you break a vow, what are the consequences?

Rinpoche: Well, the best thing to do is purify it immediately before you have to worry about the consequences. For example, let's say you are doing the nyungne, and on the day you are not supposed to drink anything you instinctively have a glass of water before you realize what you have done. If you then immediately recite the hundred-syllable mantra of Vajrasattva you can purify it and you will not have to experience the negative results of the violation. For example, it happens all the time during nyungnes that on the second day when you are not allowed to talk at all you forget the rule and say something because normally you are in the habit of talking all the time. If, when you do that, you immediately confess it, it will not be a problem. On the other hand, if you do something that breaks the rules out of conscious disrespect, it is completely different. If you take the attitude, "It doesn't matter, who cares if I break these vows?" it is much harder to purify.

Question: Where do jokes fit in during the nyungne? Some might seem like lies — or is that alright?

Rinpoche: The problem with jokes is not that they violate the vow against lying. They violate the vow against coquettish behavior. They are considered play so they are considered in the category of singing, dancing, and playing musical instruments. Therefore there should be no joking during a nyungne.

Question: On that same topic, in avoiding coquettish behavior you said that included anything playful. Would that include video games, sports, and television?

Rinpoche: Yes, all that should be completely avoided during the nyungne.

Question: I wonder if you could clarify a little more about the hinayana, mahayana, and vajrayana aspect of the nyungne practice. You said a certain aspect of the vows is hinayana but then you also said it is in a mahayana context. And then isn't the practice vajrayana?

Rinpoche: What Khenpo Karthar Rinpoche usually says about that is that the meditation practice is vajrayana, the motivation for both meditation and moral discipline is the bodhicitta of the mahayana, and the actual observance of the moral discipline is according to the common vehicle (hinayana). Because the vows are motivated by bodhicitta, even though you take them for twenty-four hours and the vows expire at the end of that time, the seed is nevertheless maintained in your continuum. That is why you can repeat the practice in the future after receiving the vows from a preceptor once.

Question: Does the empowerment of Thousand-Armed Chenrezig only apply to the nyungne practice or does receiving one Chenrezig empowerment permit you to do any Chenrezig practice?

Rinpoche: They are different empowerments, so you should get the Four-Armed Chenrezig empowerment in order to do that practice. However, when people are doing either Four-Armed Chenrezig or nyungne as a group practice it is permitted to do the practice as long as one person there has had the empowerment. However, if you are doing such practices individually, the requirement would be that you must have received the empowerment, transmission, and practice instructions.

Question: My experience with nyungnes has been with a preceptor, and a little bit of the teaching today almost sounded like do-it-yourself instructions. How does one give oneself sojong vows and so forth?

Rinpoche: The viewpoint of the text on this point is that the first time someone does a nyungne or takes these sojong vows, they must take them from a preceptor. This person may be a fully ordained monastic, a novice monastic, or a lay preceptor, but they must hold the lineage of these vows. Then, having received them once from a preceptor, if you thereafter do the practice on your own you can do it without a preceptor. Practically speaking, almost invariably when it is done as a group practice there will be a preceptor present, and in that case even if you have already done the practice you do take the vows again from the preceptor. However it is not necessarily the case that you are going to have access to a preceptor when you do it as an individual practice. If you do it in personal retreat or if you wish to do it on certain auspicious occasions on your own, then you do not need a preceptor, provided you have done it with a preceptor before. You simply repeat the vows in the same posture and in the same way as you would with a preceptor present. Visualizing the Bodhisattva Chenrezig and all buddhas and bodhisattvas in the sky in front of you, you take the vows from them.

Question: If you have broken one of the lay precepts, what do you do? Can it be repaired? What are the consequences of breaking the vow?

Rinpoche: Whenever a vow that has been undertaken is broken, you should go to the preceptor and explain the circumstances in as much detail as necessary. Then the preceptor will inform you of an appropriate manner of restitution and purification. Applying those instructions in conjunction with the four powers will take care of it. Having done restitution and so forth, if you thereafter wish to retake the vow that is up to you and the preceptor. There is no necessity that you do so. The act of reparation does not itself require that you retake the vow in order to purify it. In fact, it may not be advisable to do so. After all, if you broke it once you might break it again. Therefore you might not want to retake it, but you certainly can.

Question: I read the section of Khenpo Karthar Rinpoche's *Dharma Paths* about the lay precepts, and my sense was that if you know for a fact that you might break a vow then it is best not to take it. I have some uncertainty as to what I should do concerning lay vows. For example, I have a beer every now and then.

Rinpoche: I will give a general introduction to the topic of lay (upasaka) vows, since people have a lot of questions about them. To begin with, in the Buddhist tradition the point of taking the vows of moral discipline is the view that moral discipline is the only possible karmic cause of higher rebirth and liberation. What we are trying to do is attain buddhahood, and in order to do that we need to continue to enjoy human or divine rebirth as the basis for pursuing the spiritual path. Thus, we need to undertake and preserve some kind of moral discipline. This is the primary reason that the Buddha introduced the whole tradition of vows and ordination. Nevertheless, within the general category of vows there are many different styles that are appropriate to different individuals. There are some who wish to devote their entire lives to spirituality to the exclusion of everything else. For such persons there is monastic ordination, which includes both full and novice ordination.

There are also many householders who have families and the financial responsibilities that go along with that. Such people have less freedom to devote themselves to Dharma. Nevertheless, a layperson will still want to obtain a fortunate rebirth so they can achieve awakening. Regardless of our lifestyle, we need to continue taking incarnation in the human realm because a human body is simply the best container for the spiritual path. As a human being, you can traverse the entire path from the initial generation of bodhicitta until the attainment of full awakening. For the benefit of those who are householders, there exists the lifelong lay or upasaka ordination and the temporary ordination of the sojong vows.

There are five lay vows. It is not the case that anyone who is ordained as an upasaka is required to take all five. The ceremony leaves a choice and it is entirely up to you how many and which of the vows you wish to take. The five are the four root vows: no killing, no stealing, no lies about spiritual attainment, and no adultery, and there is also the branch vow, which is the vow not to consume intoxicants. You can take any one of these vows, and any combination of two, three, or four of them, up to the complete set of five. In the mahayana tradition, there are no temporary vows with the exception of the sojong vows. You are taking them for the duration of your life. Therefore you need to consider carefully which ones you feel confident you can keep. It is best to only take those you are quite confident you will be able to keep.

Using what you asked about as an example, if someone who consumes intoxicants does not see that as particularly posing a problem for them, but they nevertheless feel the wish to occasionally consume them or feel socially required to consume them, then the answer is simply not to take that particular vow.

Question: I am unclear on the sexual misconduct vow. Is it appropriate for persons who are not married?

Rinpoche: Basically the four root vows are the foundation of all Buddhist moral discipline, and in the case of a householder the vow pertaining to sex is not to commit adultery. To answer your question as simply as possible, if you are not married, or if you are married but you are not sure about what is happening with your marriage, you are better off not taking it. The essence of this vow is a lifelong commitment to your partner. Therefore it is only appropriate to take the vow if you feel an unchanging and unconditional commitment to your partner.

Question: If direct access to the preceptor from whom one has taken the lay vows is not available, is there any way to temporarily repair the negative karma that occurs from breaking it?

Rinpoche: If it is impossible to make direct contact with the preceptor from whom you received the vow, until that becomes possible you should imagine the Bodhisattva

Rest for the Fortunate

Chenrezig in the sky in front of you and admit the infraction or violation while invoking the four powers of confession and restitution. That is enough.

Question: I have been thinking about the question of killing, and realizing that there are many ways we could be involved with killing someone. There might be a case where someone or a group of people eats up all the food in a certain place so that somebody else starves. When my grandmother was dying, we gave her morphine to take her out of her pain, knowing that it would shut her system down. My question is, how far do you go regarding not killing?

Rinpoche: Your question is about the vow not to kill, but by extension it also brings up certain general issues about all of the vows. First of all, there is a significant difference in the strictness between the twenty-four-hour vows and the lifelong vows. Because the day-long vows are only taken or renewed for one day, they are much stricter.

As we have also seen, to break any of the upasaka vows, four elements have to be present in the action. These are the basis, intention, execution, and completion. To cover these in more detail, the basis means that you have to correctly recognize the basis of the action which is going to violate the vow. For example, in order to break the vow not to kill, you have to generate the intention to kill someone and recognize that they are a human being. The intention is that you actually have to want to kill them. Killing them accidentally does not break the vow. The execution is that you actually do something. Simply wanting to kill them does not break the vow. You have to either do something or tell someone else to do it. Then completion means that it happens to work. The person actually dies. If all four of these are not present, while it is a violation, it does not actually break the vow. This is true for all five of them. For any of the vows to be broken, there has to be all four of these components present.

Bardor Tulku Rinpoche

In your particular question about the vow not to kill, you used the example of someone who is terminally ill and on medication, where the medication itself becomes the cause of that person's demise. Whether or not the vow was broken depends upon how the medication causes that person's death. There are several possibilities. One is if the person administering the medication is doing so according to the physician's prescription and does not exceed it, and therefore is simply trying to remove the other person's pain. If their intention is not to end the person's life, then they have not broken the vow.

There also might be the case where through carelessness or through getting mixed up you exceed the prescription and the person dies accidentally. Since there was no intention, you have not broken the vow in this case.

The third case is deliberate euthanasia, where you intentionally increase the medication or give new medication in order to "put the person to sleep." Buddhism forbids this. It is considered permissible to take someone off life support if it is their clear wish, but it is not permissible to intentionally give medication or increase medication to actively kill them. Doing so would break the vow not to kill.

Question: Is there a set of prayers to say for people who have died or are dying if they are not Buddhists?

Rinpoche: You can use Buddhist prayers to pray for the benefit of someone who is not Buddhist. It does not matter whether the person you are praying for is Buddhist or not, because they still want to be happy and not suffer. If you are praying for someone who is already deceased, the most commonly recommended practices are Chenrezig and Amitabha. In both cases you would dedicate the merit of the practice to the purification of wrongdoing and obscurations and the fortunate rebirth of the deceased. In the case of the Amitabha practice, you would dedicate the merit of the practice not only to the purification of that person, but to their rebirth in the realm of Amitabha, the realm of Sukhavati. In addition, if you feel the person's primary need is for purification, then you can do something like the confession to the Thirty-Five Buddhas and dedicate it to that purpose. The Vajrasattva practice can also be used to accomplish their purification.

If someone is still alive and in the midst of serious illness or afflicted by other problems, the most commonly used liturgies are the Tara practices, either green or white. However, the most important thing is that you do a practice with which you are familiar so that you can do it effectively. Since the essence of all the deities is the same, any practice with which you are comfortable can benefit the person.

Question: When you talked about the hell realms, you described many things such as being burned and so on. These were things that I had not thought were part of the Buddhist doctrine. Could you tell us more about that?

Rinpoche: There is a custom in the Buddhist tradition of talking a great deal about hell and getting specific about all sorts of gory sufferings. I will give a general explanation of hell realms from a Buddhist perspective. Hell is regarded as a form of rebirth external to the human realm that is extremely unpleasant. It results from negative actions. It is not understood to be permanent or to be a punishment imposed by any form of deity or creative force.

Hell is not understood as any type of punishment or imposition because there is no being who has the ability to control any other being's destiny in that way. There is no notion that buddhas or bodhisattvas are sending beings to some kind of hell. On the contrary, buddhas and bodhisattvas are only concerned with the happiness of others, and they want all beings to possess all manner of happiness. This even includes types of happiness that we would almost consider trivial or insignificant. They want all beings to be free of all types of suffering, even types of suffering that we would regard as minor irritations.

Even when a being harms a buddha or a bodhisattva, they still lead that being to liberation. Therefore it is said that if you form a positive connection with a buddha or bodhisattva, that connection brings buddhahood in one lifetime, and if you form a negative connection it at least brings about the eventual end of cyclic existence for you. Even though you may suffer as a result of your actions, because of your connection with them, the buddha or bodhisattva you have harmed is going to bring you to liberation, because they are the embodiment of limitless, unbiased compassion.

There is no external being that can control your destiny, and the various types of rebirth spoken of in Buddhism, including hell, are not considered to be punishment. These types of experiences come from the imprints of our actions. What casts us into rebirth is karma. Every time we do something it forms a karmic imprint in our minds, and that imprint manifests as the tendency to take a certain type of rebirth in the future. Rebirth is not an imposition upon us. It is simply the automatic result of the actions we have engaged in. For example, even within the context of this human world we see tremendous differences in the circumstances in which people are born. Some are rich, some are poor. Some have strong constitutions and some have weak constitutions, and any combination of the above can occur. All of this is the result of those beings' previous actions.

Question: Are cigarettes considered an intoxicant? What about prescription drugs?

Rinpoche: To answer your first question, tobacco is not considered an intoxicant in the Buddhist tradition. Opium, cannabis, or any other recreational drug would violate the vow, but tobacco would not. Prescription drugs would not be considered intoxicants either, assuming you are taking them lawfully and with a prescription.

Question: Will you be a little more specific about the issue of abortion as it relates to the vow against killing? Would it be considered a bending or breaking of the precept to support the pro-choice movement? What about actually having an abortion?

Rinpoche: Performing an abortion or having an abortion yourself would violate the vow if you have taken the vow not to kill. This can be said clearly, because in the vinaya, the Buddhist teachings which are the source of these vows, it talks about abortion. When the vow against killing is defined, it refers to "a human being or that which is becoming a human being." Therefore a fetus from any point after conception until birth is governed by the vow. As far as how the vow relates to your opinion or political support of the pro-choice or pro-life movement, that is entirely up to you. Supporting either side, or neither, is a personal decision that does not conflict with the vow.

Question: How can we maintain a sense of selflessness in doing the nyungne practice without some sort of ego-clinging to the benefits? In other words, how can we avoid thinking, "By doing this I will get such and such positive outcome for myself?"

Rinpoche: The type of selfishness we give rise to when we consider the benefits of a practice like the nyungne is not considered to be a big problem. The reason for this is that when we say we are practicing or cultivating the path, implicit in that is the admission of imperfection. We are not trying or hoping to instantaneously eradicate all trace of self-interest from our pursuit of the path. We have to admit that we need some kind of motivation, some kind of enthusiasm, and to some extent that motivation or enthusiasm will be born from confidence in future benefits to oneself from the practices we are doing. The approach we take is not to attempt to get rid of that, but to extend ourselves beyond that by introducing empathy for others into the self-interest. You do that by thinking, "Just as I want such and such benefits and am therefore performing this practice of nyungne, so do all beings want to be happy and be free of suffering. Therefore I will do this practice of nyungne so that I can bring not only myself but all beings to the state of complete happiness, the state of Chenrezig." By expanding our attitude beyond mere selfish motivation in that way, it is no longer a problem.

Question: What happens if you do not break a vow, but for a moment you think that you would like to break it? Since I think that I may have those kinds of thoughts, what sort of restitution can I make?

Rinpoche: It is not a big deal, but if you want to chant the hundred-syllable mantra of Vajrasattva, that's enough.

Question: To what extent is it beneficial to sort of have a mantra floating through your head? I have gotten into that habit, and I was wondering if it was beneficial. For example, sometimes I do so when I am driving my car.

Rinpoche: It is helpful.

Question: I find it very easy to motivate myself to practice when life is not going very well. But it is more difficult to motivate myself when everything is going great and I am really happy, and it is very difficult to put that happiness aside and go sit. I wonder if there is any advice you could give to help motivate me. Or do I just need to work on being a little more unhappy?

Rinpoche: Human life is the best situation for Dharma practice. In contrast with human life, if you are born in any of the three lower states, you do not have the opportunity to practice at all, largely because you are simply too miserable. On the other hand, if you are born as a deva, a god, you are simply having too much fun to practice. One of the things that makes human life so unique is that it is a mixture of happiness and freedom on the one hand, and misery and adversity on the other. Even though we may forget to practice when we are happy because we forget why we should practice, happiness never really lasts too long. Sooner or later something happens, something goes wrong that reminds us.

However, the way to deal with the problem of sporadic practice is to cultivate a habit of practicing. We are creatures of habit to the extent that once something is habitual for us it is automatic to do it. Therefore, if you find that you practice when experiencing adversity but not when things are going well, all that means is that you have not yet made a strong habit of practicing. For example, no one needs to tell us to eat or get dressed. No one needs to remind us to change our clothes when the weather changes and so on, if for no other reason than we are used to doing such things. In the same way, the initial problem that faces us when we begin to practice Dharma is finding how to cultivate a habit and reinforce that habit until that habit is self-sustaining.

Sometimes what happens is that when people first start to practice, they practice with such diligence that they exhaust themselves and then have an aversion for practice after that. Another thing that can happen is that people are too casual about it, and so they simply do not get around to practicing. It is necessary to consciously reinforce the activity of practicing until it becomes habitual and therefore automatic. The best way to do that is to practice for exactly the same amount of time every day — whether it is fifteen minutes, a half hour, an hour, or whatever — and make sure that you keep on doing that same amount of practice every day until enough time, whether it is months or years, has passed, so that there is no longer any conscious separation between you and your practice. At that point, it is automatic. It is just part of your life and maintaining it does not require any effort.

PART TWO

The Qualities of Chenrezig

The second part of our source text *Rest for the Fortunate* has two sections. The first describes the qualities of Chenrezig.

Ultimately speaking, the Bodhisattva Chenrezig is the source of emanation of all buddhas. That means that while he is presented mainly as a bodhisattva, in actuality he is not only a buddha but is the source of emanation of all other buddhas. Therefore he embodies the three kayas (bodies) of enlightenment. As dharmakaya he is the Buddha Amitabha. As sambhogakaya he is known as the King of Space and is also called the Glacial Lake, the central sambhogakaya buddha. According to the tantra entitled *The Lotus Net*, his main nirmanakaya is called The Roar of the Lion, and there are many other nirmanakayas as well. In fact, there are said to be at least ten million major nirmanakaya forms of Chenrezig. These include the 1,002 buddhas of this fortunate eon.

Because Chenrezig is the embodiment of compassion, the displays of his compassion are as numerous as sentient beings. Wherever there is space, there are sentient beings. All of these sentient beings have their own individual problems and needs. For as long as all beings have not been liberated, the activity of the emanations of Chenrezig will continue, and they will be as numerous and as manifold as the needs of beings.

Another way to look at the various aspects of Chenrezig is to consider his body, speech, mind, qualities, and activity aspects. The body aspect of Chenrezig is the eleven-faced, thousand-armed form, which is the form of the deity with which the nyungne practice is principally concerned. The speech aspect of Chenrezig is the six-syllable mantra *om mani peme hung*. This means two things: first, that the mantra itself is the speech of the deity, and also it refers to a specific form of Chenrezig, which is known as "The One of the Six Syllables." The mind aspect or mind emanation of the Bodhisattva Chenrezig is the wisdom protector, Six-Armed Mahakala. The emanation of his qualities is the deity Hayagriva. The emanations of Chenrezig's activity are the various forms of Tara, such as Green Tara, White Tara, and so forth.

In this way, through producing and displaying so many emanations and forms, this deity benefits beings in general, and in particular has served as the predominant deity of Tibetan Buddhism.

The scriptural sources for these statements are a group of twenty-one teachings by the Buddha. Some of these are classified as sutras and others as tantras, but all of them are concerned primarily with Chenrezig. These sutras and tantras describe the benefits of even just hearing the name of this deity as being immeasurable. It is not possible to go through all of the benefits of the deity because they are so extensive and inconceivable. To at least give you some idea of the benefits that result from any kind of contact with or supplication of this deity, there is a statement by the Buddha in the *Box Sutra* (the word box refers to a jewel box), which is one of the best-known sutras concerning Chenrezig:

> If a child of good family were to venerate all of the buddhas there are in their own places, all of the buddhas who have vanquished the enemy of ignorance, and offered to all of these buddhas fine fabrics, food, seats, bedding, medicine, and various useful and pleasant things even for eons, not only would that person not accumulate even a fraction of the merit of the Bodhisattva Chenrezig, but during all those eons of receiving those offerings, all of those buddhas could not finish enumerating the merit of this bodhisattva. It need not be said that I *[Buddha Shakyamuni]* while abiding in this world cannot com-

plete a description of Chenrezig's qualities. In short, anyone who recollects the name of this bodhisattva will be happy. They will become free from aging, sickness, death, and all suffering. There will be an end to samsara for them and they will be freed from all suffering, even while wearing white or gray clothing. *[The reference to white or gray clothing means that they are not necessarily monastics. In India, people wore white clothing if they were not monastics, so the Buddha is saying "even if they are lay people."]* By recollecting this bodhisattva, they will fly to the realm of Sukhavati, the realm of the Buddha Amitabha, as surely and swiftly as geese flying south for the winter. Having reached that realm, they will hear the Dharma directly from the Buddha Amitabha. They will abide in that realm and their bodies will be without any kind of samsaric suffering there. They will be without attachment or aversion. They will not experience apathy, nor will they experience sickness, aging, or death. In short, they will not experience any of the sufferings that begin with being born in a womb. They will be born miraculously in that realm in lotus flowers and they will be inspired to emerge from the flower by the scent of the Dharma. They will abide in that realm continually, with their minds completely entrusted to the Bodhisattva Chenrezig, and they will remain in that realm for as long as all beings without exception have not been liberated.

Additional benefits are taught in this sutra and elsewhere as well. For example, it is said that by recollecting the name of this bodhisattva, you will be immediately freed from the sufferings of sickness, demonic disturbances, fire, water, enemies, thieves, poisons, weapons, carnivorous animals, and so forth. These kinds of things are traditionally called the eight and sixteen dangers. In short, as we have said, the Bodhisattva Chenrezig is the source of emanation of all buddhas. Therefore he embodies in a single form all of the qualities of the buddhas. There is no limit on the types of emanations that he produces. Chenrezig manifests his activity by emanating not only as apparently sentient beings but also as apparently inanimate objects, such as boats, bridges, food, and medicine. It could even mean the appearance of fireflies to illuminate the path for those who have lost their way.

Chenrezig continually engages in unceasing and varied means of benefiting sentient beings. His activity is inconceivable in that he has resolved never to pass into nirvana until each and every being has achieved full awakening. In sum, all of the qualities described in all of the sutras and tantras are ultimately describing the qualities of this single bodhisattva, Chenrezig.

The Tradition and Practice of Nyungne

Next comes the second section, which has five topics. The first topic is an explanation of where the nyungne fits in with the various vehicles of Buddhist practice, and therefore what its scriptural sources are. Then there is a brief history of the lineage of this practice, followed by a general explanation of how much of the practice needs to be done. After that there is an extensive explanation of its benefits, and finally an explanation of the commitments or rules connected with nyungne.

Nyungne in the Context of the Buddhist Vehicles

There are innumerable lineages of the practices of the Bodhisattva Chenrezig. These are based upon the sutras and on the *dharanis*, which are brief texts that give the dharani or longer mantra of this deity. The lineages have come from both oral tradition and discovered teachings called terma. They can also be connected with any of the four levels of tantra (the kriya, charya, yoga, and highest yoga tantras).

The lineage of the nyungne itself is essentially drawn from the kriya tantra. Within the kriya tantra there are what are called the "three supermundane families," namely the buddha, vajra, and padma families, and there are also the three mundane families. From among these three types or families of kriya tantra, the nyungne practice is based upon the padma or lotus family of kriya tantra, and it is mainly based upon a kriya tantra called *The Dharani of the Eleven-Faced Chenrezig*.

The Lineage of Nyungne

The next topic tells the life stories of the lineage holders of this practice in order to give us an idea how effective this practice has been historically. The first person in the lineage is the great siddha and monastic Lakshminkara, who is sometimes just called Palmo, or Gelongma Palmo. We went over the story of her life at the beginning of the book, so now we will continue with her spiritual successors in the nyungne lineage.

Lakshminkara's principal disciple and holder of her lineage was a *pandita* (a greatly knowledgable scholar) who was called Dawa Shunnu or Youthful Moon. He was born in Western India in a Brahmin family. Initially he trained himself thoroughly in the various traditional areas of knowledge such as linguistics and logic, and he acquired a good reputation for scholarship. Then he took monastic ordination and eventually began to practice intensive meditation in order to realize the meaning of all the things he had studied. Because of his tremendous exertion, both while studying and later when practicing meditation, he became afflicted by an imbalance of the winds (or internal energies) which is produced by excessively rigid concentration. He resorted to all the traditional remedies for this affliction, but nothing helped. Finally he went to meet the Bhikshuni Lakshmi to request her blessing. Simply through receiving her blessing, he was cured of his ailment.

She told him that the ailment was the karmic result of his having previously upset one of his teachers, but that after having done so he had confessed his fault. She explained that because of his confession, the final outcome of the sickness was not negative because it had led him to come to meet her. She bestowed upon him the instructions of the Eleven-Faced Chenrezig. Immediately after receiving them, he achieved the supreme attainment of mahamudra on the basis of those instructions.

Dawa Shunnu's main disciple was actually a disciple both of him and his own master, Lakshminkara. He was also a pandita, and was named Jnanabhadra or Excellent Wisdom. Like Dawa Shunnu, he was born in India in the nobility, and took monastic ordination and became learned in the five sciences. In his case, because of the karmic ripening of his previous actions, he became afflicted by an ailment that was characterized by ulcerous sores covering his upper body. He applied all kinds of treatments for this, and nothing helped. Then he thought, "Well, it must be an affliction by some kind of spirit or ghost." Intending to remedy this, he obtained teachings on the wrathful deity Yamantaka from a siddha and did that practice. However, instead of reversing the affliction, it actually got three times worse.

His entire body became completely covered with infected blisters and felt intolerably hot, as though he were burning. To relieve this burning sensation he had to constantly sit in a pool of cool water. Eventually the water would get hot and start to boil, so he would have to regularly replace it with more cool water. He sought the help of everyone in the area who was known to have magical power for healing sickness, but no one was able to help him. Finally he requested the assistance of the pandita, Dawa Shunnu.

When Dawa Shunnu was on his way to help Jnanabhadra, he had a vision of Arya Tara. She told him that Jnanabhadra had previously broken his samaya with one of his teachers, and the illness was the karmic maturation of that. Tara said, "You will not be able to heal him. However, if you supplicate Lakshminkara, she can help him." Therefore Dawa Shunnu requested Lakshminkara's help on behalf of

Jnanabhadra, and together they went to Jnanabhadra. He requested their blessings, and simply through having received their blessings (primarily through that of Lakshminkara herself) his illness was completely cured.

Jnanabhadra perceived Lakshmi as Eleven-Faced Chenrezig. Thereupon she gave him concise instructions on the Chenrezig meditation practice. It was from her disciple Dawa Shunnu, however, that he received extensive instructions on the practice such as the explanations of the tantra and the elaborate form of the sadhana. Having received all the instructions, Jnanabhadra practiced them for three months as a nyungne practice. His body was transformed into an actual form of Chenrezig and he attained supreme siddhi.

His successor in the lineage was called Penyawa, who was born in the nobility of Nepal and was also a great scholar. He received a prophesy from the Bodhisattva Manjushri that he should go to India. There he received the instructions of the Eleven-Faced Chenrezig from Jnanabhadra. He practiced these for five years while begging for his sustenance. At the end of this time he had a vision of the deity, attained the supreme siddhi, and his body dissolved into rainbow light.

Penyawa's disciple is one of the best-known figures in the nyungne lineage. He is usually called the Bodhisattva Dawa Gyaltsen and is renowned as having been an incarnation of Chenrezig himself. He became the teacher of many people who were already renowned as scholars and siddhas because they received prophesies directly from the Bodhisattva Chenrezig that they should study with him. Therefore you will find mention of him in the biographies of other masters of the time.

It is most likely that Dawa Gyaltsen was Tibetan, and this would mean that he was the first Tibetan in the lineage. We can conclude that because his life story says that he prayed for seven days in front of an image of Chenrezig in Chirong, which is in Tibet. While praying for those seven days, he made the aspiration and request to Thousand-Armed Chenrezig that he be able to give eyes to one hundred who were blind, build a hundred temples, make passable a hundred dangerous roads, and support or feed a hundred monastics. He then received a prophesy from the deity that all of these aspirations would be accomplished and that he would quickly attain perfect awakening.

After that, together with a retinue of four monks, he went begging. Because of his virtue and noble aspirations he had so much merit that he acquired a great deal of wealth by begging. With that, he was able to build more than one hundred temples. He was also able to ransom the lives of more than three hundred beings and three hundred sets of eyes. "Ransoming lives" could refer to either human beings or animals. It means that he paid to free people who were going to be executed, or that he bought animals that were going to be butchered and set them free. The "ransoming of eyes" refers to the standard criminal punishment in those times of cutting out people's eyes for various crimes. He would pay off the people who were going to do this, and someone would be spared that punishment. Thus, in that way he realized his aspiration to give eyes to those who would otherwise be blind. He also used his funds to build roads through dangerous places where people were frequently killed in accidents. He also was able to support a community of about twelve hundred monastics. In short, he accomplished a great deal of virtuous activity.

There is one story about Dawa Gyaltsen that became very well known. Once when he was traveling in the area around the border of Nepal and Tibet, he came across a woman who was old and very ill. She requested his blessing, so he performed a torma ritual and made dedication prayers for her. He said to her that illness is primarily the ripening of previous negative karma, so we need to cultivate both patience and bodhicitta. She was inspired by what he said and started to cry. She said, "Never mind my previous lives. In this life I have done a lot of bad things." He said, "If you admit all of the bad things you have done that you can remember, they will be purified." In response to that she told this story:

> In Chirong I became the wife of a wealthy merchant. We had one son. When our son was seven years of age, my husband went south to Nepal to sell and trade. He was not planning to come back for three years. He left me behind, and at that point in my life I was very attractive and also I was very emotional and so I got into a relationship with another man. We had a child, which I killed. During that time, because I was supporting this other man, we used up about half of the wealth that my husband had left behind. Our son said, "What's going to happen to you when my father gets back?" I got angry when he said that. I hit him with a stone in the liver and he bled from the mouth and died. I convinced everyone that he had died of a stroke and in that way I told a lot of lies to cover up what I had been doing. We had a household priest, someone who would recite scriptures and so on for the benefit of the family, who knew the truth of what was happening, so I poisoned him and he also died.
>
> Eventually my husband, bearing a huge amount of wealth, arrived home. A servant who knew all that had happened told my husband everything. He said to her, "For tonight, pretend you don't know anything, and tomorrow I'll take out her eyes." I was listening and I heard him say this. Terrified about what was going to be done to me the next day, I poured a lot of poison into the household liquor. As a result, my husband and his seven employees, as well as two men who were our neighbors and two household servants who drank this were all poisoned. By dawn the next day they were unable to speak and they all died within two days. Not being able to conceal this at that point, I fled south to Nepal. Because I fled and they couldn't catch me, the other members of my

husband's family took revenge on my own family, so more people were killed. Since then, I have done a lot of bad things in business. I've cheated people a lot. I've done all that—now please take care of me with your compassion.

When he heard this story the Bodhisattva Dawa Gyaltsen said, "How could one woman do all of that?" He cried a long time. He said to her, "Well, Chenrezig has promised that anyone who does even one nyungne will not be reborn in the lower realms. There is nothing more powerful and nothing better than that in which to place your hopes."

He asked her to do eight nyungnes. Through his compassion and blessing, her illness became somewhat better. She performed the eight nyungnes in the fourth month, the Saga month. One night, however, she got extremely thirsty and broke down and had some liquor. One other time she got extremely hungry and ate two of the four food tormas that she had offered on the shrine. Thus she did two imperfect nyungnes and six good ones. Still, she completed the eight nyungnes and not long after that she died.

Some time later, Dawa Gyaltsen was bestowing the bodhisattva vow and teaching about it. At that time, a mundane deity or spirit named Tsimara appeared to everyone and said to the bodhisattva, "Show some sign of your attainment." In response to that, the first thing Dawa Gyaltsen did was to reveal an eye which was openly staring in the palm of his hand, just as Chenrezig has eyes on all the palms of his thousand hands. Everybody saw that, and some people also saw his body in the form of the Eleven-Faced Chenrezig. Some saw him as as the Four-Armed Chenrezig, and some as the two-armed form, and so on. When the spirit Tsimara saw this he was very inspired, and promised to protect the teachings of the nyungne.

Because of the miracles he had demonstrated, everyone around Dawa Gyaltsen developed great faith in him, and many openly confessed their own past wrongdoing. One of these people was a monk, and he also asked the bodhisattva, "Remember that old woman last year who had killed fifteen people? I heard she died. Where has she been reborn?" The bodhisattva smiled and said:

> The benefits of the nyungne practice of the Eleven-Faced Chenrezig are immeasurable. However there are very few people who are able to actually do it. That woman was reborn in eastern India as the child of an affluent Brahmin family. She is there now adorned with a great deal of beautiful jewelry. She has been reborn as a human being because she did those nyungnes. However, because one night she drank some liquor out of thirst she has some mental problems such that she has a great deal of highs and lows in her mind. *[Probably today we would call her bipolar]*. As well, because she ate two food tormas when she was not supposed to eat anything, the person she has been reborn as is not very attractive. However, in this life she will continue the practice of Chenrezig and immediately after her death this time she will be reborn in Sukhavati. Anyone who has done eight nyungnes and has recited the name of the Bodhisattva Chenrezig a hundred times while prostrating will definitely be reborn in Sukhavati and will attain an irreversible state there. Finally, they will attain full awakening. Anyone who does even one nyungne will definitely not be reborn in lower states. This Dharma is the sadhana or method of accomplishment of all buddhas and bodhisattvas. Therefore, all of you, please practice it.

Dawa Gyaltsen's principal disciple and lineage holder is called the Siddha Nyipugpa. It was not his birth name; Nyipug means the "cave of the sun," and he was given that name because that is where he eventually lived. Nyipugpa was born in Ngari in Western Tibet, and his personal name was Yitrok, which means bewitching or charming. He became a monastic, and until the age of twenty-six he studied assiduously and acquired a reputation for the purity of his monastic discipline, his learning, and his benevolence of character. Then at the age of twenty-six he had a dream in which he had a vision of Arya Tara. She said to him that in a certain region, "There is an incarnation of the Bodhisattva Chenrezig. If you go there you will accomplish benefit for yourself and for others." Having received that prophesy from Tara, he went there and met the Bodhisattva Dawa Gyaltsen, made offerings to him, and requested teachings that would be easy to practice, very beneficial, and that would guarantee he would never be reborn in the lower states. In response to that, Dawa Gyaltsen bestowed upon him the empowerment and instructions of the eleven-faced form of Chenrezig, the basis for the nyungne practice.

After receiving the instructions and empowerment, he gathered together five loads of barley flour and went to the slope of a mountain called the Taki Gangri or the Snow Mountain of Taki. He lived there for seven years doing one nyungne after another, and for food he relied only on the practice of yogic nourishment or *rasayana*. For those seven years he never had any contact with another person. No one even knew he was there. After seven years of nyungne practice he attained realization to the point where rays of light would shine out of the palms of his hands and sunlight would shine through him. In short, he started to show signs of the dissolution of the coarse elements of his physical body, the beginning of the attainment of a rainbow body. Also at that time a local deity promised to protect the teachings of the nyungne and was therefore added to the ranks of the protectors of this practice. Flying through the sky, Nyipugpa went to the cave of Nyipug, after which he is named. There he enlisted the aid of some emanated carpenters, and together with other craftsmen they built a shrine with an image of this form of Chenrezig. Because Nyipugpa lived there for the rest of his life, he is known by the name of that place.

Once while he was there and doing a nyungne, all of a sudden in the middle of the night he felt a terrible pain in his eyes, as if they were about to burst and pop right out of his head. At the same time he had a vision of Chenrezig in the form of a person who was white in color and who said to him, "Five hundred lifetimes ago you were born in southern India and were an oarsman. At that time with your oars you pierced the eyes of a fish, and this is the last trace or ripening of the karma you accumulated by doing that." Another time when he was doing a nyungne, his right cheek swelled and became inflamed and extremely painful, and at the same time he had a vision of Chenrezig who said to him, "Nine hundred lifetimes ago you threw a stone at a water buffalo and hit him on the cheek. This is the last ripening of that karma."

Nyipugpa was of great benefit to many, and for the duration of his life mostly just did one nyungne after another. Even when he was ill and could not do nyungne continuously, he did them without fail on the "three great days" of every month, which means the eighth, fifteenth, and thirtieth days of the lunar month. He received a prophesy from Chenrezig that immediately after his current life he would be reborn in the realm of Sukhavati in the West where he would attain perfect awakening. On the eighth day of the month in his seventy-seventh year, while performing the second or main day of a nyungne (and therefore he was observing silence), he passed away about halfway through the day. There were numerous auspicious signs in connection with his passing.

His principal disciple was known as Supa Dorje Gyalpo. Dorje Gyalpo means Vajra King and Supa refers to Suyu, the region where he was born. He was born with the name Tsultrim Könchog. At the age of seven his karmic connection with the mahasiddha Nyipugpa was awakened, and he met him. From Nyipugpa he received monastic ordination and gradually became extremely learned in the three vehicles — the shravakayana, the pratyekabuddhayana, and the bodhisattvayana[20] — and very noble in his conduct. His teacher Nyipugpa said to him, "For you, one practice of Dharma that is all sufficient will be enough. You do not need to do many different things." Saying that, he gave him the

Rest for the Fortunate

empowerment and instructions for the nyungne practice of Chenrezig. In response to that, Supa Dorje Gyalpo promised to continue the nyungne practice for the rest of his life. For five years after receiving the teachings, he did one nyungne after another in one residence without moving around. After having done this practice for those five years, on the eighth day of the third month of his thirty-sixth year, he had a vision of the Bodhisattva Chenrezig and received from Chenrezig the blessing that made his body, speech, and mind indistinguishable from those of Chenrezig. At that time he achieved tremendous supercognition and miraculous abilities and thereafter was able to benefit beings tremendously. For the duration of his life he lived only by begging. He never accumulated possessions, and throughout his life never tasted either liquor or meat. He did one nyungne after another until the day of his death. After he passed away, the remains of his physical body turned into *shariram*, which are tiny round crystalline relics. These relics were enshrined in a stupa which up to the time of the writing of this text was known to produce additional relics, which would be emitted from the stupa upon being supplicated or venerated.

His principal disciple was known as Shangtön Drajig, which means "Drajig, the teacher from Shang." He was born in the region of Trulpu. At the time of his birth there was an earthquake and a ferocious thunderstorm which caused someone who was the enemy of his family to become frightened and to give up his persecution of the family. That is why he was given the nickname Drajig, which means "ter-

---

20. Although the more usual modern presentation of the three vehicles of Buddhist practice is as hinayana, mahayana, and vajrayana, this is actually the more traditional categorization of the three vehicles. Pratyekabuddhas and shravakas are the two types of practitioners of individual liberation, so together these two vehicles comprise what is called hinayana. Then the mahayana vehicle of the bodhisattvas is divided into two parts, the sutrayana and tantrayana. (Tantrayana is a synonym for vajrayana.) Thus these two systems of designation cover the same material but in slightly different ways.

rified of the enemy." He became a monk and studied at the great monastery of Sakya and other places. He became very learned and famous for his knowledge of Buddhism. In his lifestyle he followed the example of the great masters of the Kadampa tradition, which means that he was extremely precise in his monastic discipline. He received a prophesy from Tara that he would found and lead a monastic institution where no less than five hundred monastics would live. He went to meet Supa Dorje Gyalpo and from him received the instructions and empowerment of Eleven-Faced Chenrezig.

Then for three years and four months he did the nyungne practice continually, one after another. At the end of that time, in the beginning of the first part of the night on the full moon day of that month, he had a vision of the Twenty-One Taras. During the second part of the same night he had a vision of the Medicine Buddha and the seven other buddhas in his retinue. In the third part of the night he had a vision of Chenrezig himself surrounded by many other deities of the kriya and charya tantras, and from these deities and especially from Chenrezig he received empowerment and blessing directly.

The deity gave him the instruction, "Child, do not eat the food of the faithful or the food of the dead. *[In other words, do not survive on offerings given from faith or offerings given for prayers on behalf of the dead.]* Rely upon solitude, live in retreat, and if possible rely upon yogic sustenance or rasayana. If you cannot do that, then at least only beg for your food and benefit beings as much as possible." In accordance with his guru's wishes and the deity's direct instructions, after living for three years in that place where he had this vision, he gave away all of his fine robes and religious articles. Without anyone knowing where he was going, he went to a hidden valley where for three months he continued to do one nyungne after another.

After three months of doing the nyungne practice in that valley, he developed a terrible fever for seven days. The fever got so high that he thought he was going to die. While he was basically waiting to die from this ailment, early one morning when he was half asleep he had another vision of Chenrezig. Chenrezig said to him, "Many lifetimes ago you were a fisherman in India, and while a fisherman you cooked many live fish in boiling water and ate them. Because of that you spent many hundreds of millions of years in the hell of boiling water, and while you were there I was able to hit you with a ray of light, causing you to be reborn as a human being. From that time until now you have had sixteen human births, during which time you have always had some connection or another with me. Now you have actually met me face to face, and this fever is the experience of the last remnants of the karma you accumulated by boiling those fish alive." Saying that, Chenrezig placed his hand on him. The fever broke, and he recovered.

However, because of the intensity of his austerity and the deprivation he underwent, he developed an imbalance of the winds and for about seventy days was almost unconscious. Probably he was in something like a coma. After that he became desperately hungry, and to sustain himself he ate whatever he could find, which was basically things like the chaff of grain, and even dust and earth, boiled in water. Sometimes he would find garbage left by shepherds and things like that. At one point he went for seven months without having so much as one drop of water. In that way he engaged in tremendous austerity for three years, and continued to meditate on the generation and completion aspects of the Chenrezig practice. At the end of that time, he attained siddhi such that he was able to fly and was able to reverse the current of rivers. In short, he came to possess all sorts of miraculous abilities. When he passed away and was cremated, from the cremation fire there were large amounts of little white relic pills (shariram), and also his tongue and heart were not burned by the fire. They were placed in two reliquaries, which still existed at the time Situ Rinpoche wrote *Rest for the Fortunate*.

His major disciple was called Jangpa Khenchen Tsidulwa, or "Great Preceptor Tsidulwa from the North." He became a monk at a young age and studied the Dharma assiduously, especially the five texts of Maitreya. He achieved the perfection of nobility of conduct and learning, and was given the name Thupgye Jangchup. He is said to have been so pure a monastic that there was almost a perfume or fine scent of morality that emanated from his body. Because he had tremendous merit, he was able to found a monastic institution which housed more than one thousand monks, and so was able to accomplish a great deal of external virtue. In accordance with a prophesy he received directly from Tara, he went to where the previous lineage holder, Shangtön Rinpoche, was living, and from him received the sadhana of Eleven-Faced Chenrezig. Thupgye Jangchup made the commitment to do one thousand nyungnes. After having done three hundred of them, on the fifteenth day of the fourth month (the month of Saga), he had a vision of Thousand-Armed Chenrezig, who gave him his blessing. At that time he attained realization. He was consequently able to bring many beings to a state of maturity and freedom. It is said that immediately after he passed away he was reborn in Sukhavati in the presence of the Bodhisattva Maitreya. In short, his life is a record of inconceivable miracles.

Tsidulwa's principal disciple is called the Dharmaraja of Sukhavati (Chögyal Dewachenpa in Tibetan). He was born in a place called Dolong, and his personal name was Shakya Jangchup. He became a monk and was diligent in study, and in particular became very learned about the vinaya. He initially relied upon Medicine Buddha and Tara as the basis of his practice. He experienced a vision of Tara in which she advised him to see Tsidulwa. From him he received the empowerment and instructions for this nyungne practice of Chenrezig, and he performed the amount of mantras required to complete the practice twenty-one times. After doing so, he returned to his birthplace where he built a monastery. There he remained, and every year thereafter for twenty years he taught a continuous series of courses on the prajnaparamita and the vinaya.

He also made the commitment to his teacher (as his teacher had done before him) to perform one thousand nyungnes. And like his teacher, after he had done the practice three hundred times he achieved realization. In his case, what happened was that on the night of the eighth day of the month (which coincided with the second day of his nyungne) he had a vision of going to the Potala, the pure realm of Chenrezig, and he saw it exactly as it is described in the sutras. He met the Bodhisattva Chenrezig, from whom he received the prophesy and blessing, and as a result was able to generate many different samadhis. After that point, he had unstoppable and unlimited signs of attainment and supercognition. Therefore he was able to benefit beings tremendously. Finally at the end of his life he went to the Potala, the realm of Chenrezig, and there were many miraculous signs attending his death.

Chögyal Dewachenpa's principal disciple was Khenchen Chuzangwa, which means "The Great Preceptor, Chuzangwa." His ordination name was Jangchup Bar or "blazing enlightenment." He demonstrated perfection in learning and, having received a prophesy from Chenrezig, he went to be in Chögyal Dewachenpa's presence. From him Khenchen Chuzangwa received the sadhana of the nyungne. In accordance with the command of his teacher, he immediately began to perform nyungnes, one after another. Like his teacher and his teacher's teacher, after three hundred successive nyungnes he attained realization. In his case, on the evening of the fifteenth day of the month, the full moon day, which coincided with the main day of the nyungne, he had a vision of Thousand-Armed Chenrezig surrounded by the gurus of the Kadampa tradition. At that point he complained to the deity, saying, "I've been meditating on you for so long. Why have I never seen you until now?" In response the deity said, "You have never been separate from me for even an instant, but when I first prophesied to you that you should go and meet your teacher you wondered if I were genuine or if I were a mara, a deception, and that doubt has prevented you from seeing me until now." Saying that, he then gave his blessing and also the instruction to benefit beings on a vast scale.

From that time onward he experienced himself as inseparable from the Bodhisattva Chenrezig, and was never without his constant guidance. Relying upon begging as a means of sustenance, he was able to sustain a monastic sangha of three hundred individuals. In this way he was able to benefit the teachings and beings greatly. When he performed the Medicine Buddha practice, he had a vision of the Eight Medicine Buddhas and was given divine ambrosia by the yaksha chieftains who are the attendants of the Medicine Buddha. When he performed the ceremony of the Sixteen Elders, he had a vision in which the Sixteen Elders actually appeared. In short, there were many miraculous events that occurred throughout his life. Once when he was teaching he made the prediction, "Three hundred years from now at this place which I have founded three signs will occur, and when they do it will be an indication that this Dharma of the nyungne will be easy to practice and therefore should be especially emphasized. This teaching is the broom with which we sweep away our obscurations."

Before he passed away he said the following to his disciples: "I'm going soon. Therefore, take the remnants of my provisions *[which he had accumulated through begging]*, and don't use them for any other virtue." Often when someone passes away they will have ceremonies commissioned for them. He said, "Don't bother doing that. Just use them to support the nyungne practice of as many people as possible. If you can, use it to feed them." By this he meant to use the food for the meal on the first day of the nyungne practice. He continued, "If you can't use it for that, then use it for the soup or the gruel that is served on the morning after the second day. If you can't do that, then use it to buy wood to feed the fires with which the gruel is cooked. In short, I have received a direct statement from Chenrezig himself that using my provisions to sustain the practice of others will be far more beneficial and far more meritorious than anything else you could do with it." He went on, "This is something that Chenrezig himself said to me. That is quite different than any statement said by a human because he never lies."

Having given that instruction, Khenchen Chuzangwa passed away. His body was left alone for a week, and during that time it started to dissolve into rainbow light. When that happens, the body actually condenses or shrinks so that it becomes smaller. Therefore after three days his body had become the size of a seven-year-old child. This was witnessed by one of his disciples who thought, "Before it disappears altogether we'd better cremate it so we can have some relics, something to pray to and sustain our faith." They cremated what was left of his body, and it became a massive bunch of shariram or relics.

Khenchen Chuzangwa's principal disciple was the lord of Dharma, Sherab Bum, who was born in Tsang. At the time of his birth there were some remarkable events that were considered auspicious. He became a monk, studied hard, and became very learned—so much so that he became an instructor in monastic academies. He was also learned in the vajrayana tantras. He practiced the six limbs of union (the completion stage practices of the Kalachakra tantra) and perfected the ten signs of the first of these six. He was also known to have attained five types of supercognition. He had a vision of the Red Manjushri and one of Tara in which she instructed him to go to Chuzangwa, the previous lineage holder, and receive the nyungne practice from him. He did so, and performed the nyungnes one after another for three months. At the end of this time he had a vision of Eleven-Faced Chenrezig surrounded by the eight Taras who offer protection from the eight dangers. From that time onward he was never separate from Chenrezig. His discernment (prajna) was extremely great. He was able to benefit beings tremendously through teaching and through practice. As with his predecessors, when he passed away many miracles occurred.

We will complete the description of the nyungne lineage with the life story of the teacher who is probably the most famous holder of this lineage aside from the Bhikshuni Lakshmi herself, namely the Bodhisattva Thogme or Ngulchu Thogme. Thogme means unstoppable, and it is the Tibetan translation of the name Asanga. However, Ngulchu Thogme is not the well-known Indian Buddhist master of that name. He was a Tibetan Kadampa master and is best known because he composed a very famous text, *The Thirty-Seven Practices of a Bodhisattva*.

He was born in Tibet in the region of Tsang. At the time of his birth there were many extraordinary signs such as an earthquake, a rain of flowers, and so forth. It is said that from a very early age—from the time he could speak, at least—it was evident that he had a natural altruistic tendency. He seemed to naturally or automatically think more about others than himself. While still a child, he worked for his family as a yak herder. While he was doing that his previous connection with the Dharma was awakened, so he left to become a monk, and studied assiduously. Every time some significant event occurred in his life there were miracles and signs accompanying it. For example, on the day of his ordination, there was a rain of flowers and many other signs during the ceremony. He was given the ordination name of Zangpo Pal, which means "glorious benevolence." He became extraordinarily learned in all of the various aspects of the teachings of the sutras, the Middle Way school, the prajnaparamita, the vinaya, the abhidharma, and so forth. In so doing, he acquired a reputation for intelligence and learning while still quite young. He settled in a place called Bhodung and established his seat there.

Ngulchu Thogme studied with about forty different teachers, many of them famous. These included Dolpopa and Duldun Rinpoche, who were lineage holders of the glorious Sakya tradition, Sangye Won of the Shangpa Kagyu tradition, the terton Rinchen Lingpa, and many others. It seems that he studied and mastered all of the teachings that had reached Tibet from India at that time. Especially, he had two teachers who were his main guides and supreme in their influence on him. From one of these, the great preceptor

Sonam Drak, the principal teaching he received was the *lojong* or mind training teachings of the mahayana. This was the basis of his main practice. Through meditating on these he generated the full attainment of both relative and absolute bodhicitta as they are described in the lojong teachings. His realization was such that he could actually take onto himself the illnesses of others. This meant that whenever he saw anyone who had problems such as a skin disease, a particularly virulent infestation of lice, or other types of chronic pain, mental problems, and so on, simply through the power of compassion they would get better and he would temporarily exhibit the symptoms of whatever had been afflicting them. He was able to make a connection with anyone he saw, such that they were benefited immediately and planted on the path to liberation.

When he first received the elaborate transmission of the bodhisattva vow, there were again many miraculous signs, including an earthquake and rainbow light appearing in the sky. From the lord of Dharma, Sherab Bum, his predecessor in the nyungne lineage, he received (among other teachings) the six limbs of union of the Kalachakra Tantra. Like his master, by meditating upon these he perfected the ten signs and the eight qualities, and thus displayed signs of attainment through that practice. However, his teacher also said to him that in fact Togme's karmically destined yidam or deity throughout many lives was the eleven-faced form of Chenrezig, and gave him the transmission of several different lineages of the deity. These included the principal lineage which comes from the Mahasiddha Lakshminkara, as well as the lineages of Nagarjuna and Chandragomen. In that way, he received the empowerments, instructions, and liturgical transmissions for all of these lineages.

He lived in the cave called the "Dharma Fortress of Mercury" or Ngulchu Chödzong, which is why he is often called Ngulchu Thogme. From that point onward he did not interact with anyone except his attendant. For twenty years, until he was in his sixties, he simply practiced the nyungne and the lojong or mind training teachings of the mahayana. He did a hundred prostrations every day as part of the nyungne, and lived in retreat combining the practices of the sutras and tantras. After the first six months he had a vision of Eleven-Faced Chenrezig surrounded by the five members of the mandala of Amoghapasha, and many other forms of that deity. He received Chenrezig's blessing, and from that point onward he generated a realization of emptiness and a motivation of compassion that were no different than those of Chenrezig himself.

A contemporary of his was Trewo Rinpoche (also known as Trewo Tubten), who was one of the primary disciples of the Third Gyalwa Karmapa Rangjung Dorje. He made a well-known remark about Ngulchu Thogme. (To understand the context for this remark you need to know that in Tibetan parlance, Chenrezig is often simply called "Great Compassion.") He said, "When we say Great Compassion, we are not really talking about this white figure that we draw on our walls. We are talking about someone who sees and loves all beings as if they were each his only child—someone who has mastered both emptiness and compassion like the Bodhisattva Thogme." This remark, which was made during the Bodhisattva Thogme's lifetime, made him quite famous.

He was someone who only thought of, and was only aware of, his own faults. He never thought about the faults of others. Therefore, when he talked about other people he always spoke only of their virtues, regardless of whether he was talking about his social superiors or inferiors. He never displayed any concern for acquisition and loss, praise and denigration, and so forth. Because he was so loving, through the power of his love any person or animal who came close to him immediately calmed down. This happened not only with domestic animals but also with wild animals and even predators. Whenever birds and cats and dogs and people of any station were around him, they immediately settled down. Even if people were involved in a dispute or if animals were natural enemies like birds and cats, they would get along when in his presence.

He continually exhibited the actual practice of the six perfections as they are traditionally taught, and was frequently known to give away anything and everything—even what he was sitting on, his clothing, and so forth. In short, he had all the signs of a genuine holy being: speaking kindly, being reliable, generous, profound in his wisdom, and able to explain the Dharma in a definitive and authoritative way. Whenever he taught, especially whenever he bestowed the bodhisattva vow, there were miraculous signs such as rains of flowers. He made the following remark to his disciples about the custom of bestowing the bodhisattva vow:

> During the days of Atisha and Geshe Dromtönpa, the bodhisattva vow was bestowed somewhat restrictively and therefore nowadays there are very few who can bestow it and very few who have had the opportunity to generate bodhicitta. Nevertheless, since that time the restrictions on the bestowing of the bodhisattva vow have been relaxed. Therefore, as many of you who are able to bestow it should please do so.

His room and his clothing always bore the fragrant scent of moral discipline, and his disciples frequently saw him in the form of the Bodhisattva Chenrezig. He had complete control over the dream state, mastery of the illusory body, and great supercognition. He bestowed the pratimoksha vow and the bodhisattva vow so often, he composed so much in terms of literary composition, he spent so much of his life in isolated retreat, and so many of his disciples became siddhas that you would think he had spent his whole life doing any one of these things—ordaining people, writing, being in retreat, or teaching. During his lifetime, all of the best-known teachers of all lineages throughout Tibet studied with him. People who spoke many different languages from the Himalayan region came to learn from him. All of those who contacted him, who saw him, who heard him, who thought of him, and who touched him were ripened and brought to the state of eventual liberation. He passed away in the bird year on the evening of the twentieth day of the ninth month, and in the midst of many miracles he dissolved into the heart of Chenrezig.

Up until Ngulchu Thogme, the lineage was basically one to one from Lakshmi, but because he was such a prominent teacher he had an inconceivable number of disciples. In the Jonang tradition he had a lineage that was passed down from Kuntuzangpo and his successors. This was the source of one tradition of the nyungne in the Karma Kagyu tradition, which used a liturgical composition by Karma Chagme Rinpoche based on the teachings of that tradition. In general, through his activity the nyungne practice really spread into all lineages, such that each of the various traditions has one or several longer and shorter forms of the nyungne practice. We consider him the last member of the lineage not because it ended with him, but because he was the person who propagated it so widely that it is now part of all lineages of Tibetan Buddhism.

There are various traditions of the practice that come from Ngulchu Thogme, such as the nyungne ritual that was composed by the great Vidyadhara Tsewang Norbu of Khatok. This comes from the Jonang tradition of nyungne. A great bodhisattva named Drakar Sonam Rinchen established a tradition that went down to Kunga Drolchog and to Taranatha and so on. In short, because of Thogme's activity, the nyungne exists as an unbroken lineage with unimpaired blessings down to the present day.

When and How to Practice Nyungne

Now we turn to the third topic, which is an explanation of when and how much to practice nyungne. The first question is when to do it. In general it can be done, of course, at any time. However, it is especially recommended that it be done on the four great yearly occasions of the Buddhist calendar and the other occasions that have been described in earlier parts of this book. In particular, because Lakshmi herself and most of the gurus of this lineage attained siddhi during the fourth month, the Saga month, that is considered to be the most auspicious time to do it because it embodies the greatest blessing. It is taught that if you do a nyungne during the fourth month of the Buddhist lunar calendar, attainment will come quickly and there will be no obstacles to that attainment.

The second question is how much to do it. As is usually the case with yidam practice, there are three ways to appraise the measure of the practice. These are: by time, by number, and by indications.

Time refers to how long (i.e., how many days) is spent on the practice. The general time requirement is to do eight nyungnes, one after another. That takes seventeen days. Each nyungne has a preliminary day and a main day, and then after the sixteen days the next morning is spent completing the practice. This period of time spent doing eight full nyungnes is called "the eightfold virtue" and is the standard amount of time required to complete the practice.

The second measure of the practice is number, which refers to the number of mantras to be recited. If it is measured by number, the long dharani should be recited at least forty thousand times, the short dharani a hundred thousand times, and the essence mantra, *om mani peme hung*, six hundred thousand times. In the longer form of the practice there are additional mantras that do not occur in the form of the practice that we do. If you do this longer form, then the dharani of the wish-fulfilling wheel would be done one thousand times and the dharanis of the ten bhumis and of the boundless gates would be done as much as is appropriate.

The third way of appraising or measuring the practice is by indication, which refers to signs of realization. These signs are clearly presented in the history of the lineage, which describes the particular signs of success or realization that came about from the practice of the lineage gurus. If you were to measure your practice in terms of signs, you would continue the practice indefinitely regardless of how long or how many mantras you recite until you achieve clear signs of realization. Optimally, this would consist of meeting the deity face to face and receiving prophesy and empowerment from him. If that is not attained, at least there should be a clear indication in actual experience, visions, and/or dreams of the attainment of realization.

Further Statements on the Benefits of Nyungne

Next we come to the fourth topic, which is a detailed explanation of the benefits of doing the nyungne practice. There are eight points discussed in this part of the text.

Chenrezig's Statements on the Benefit of Nyungne

We begin with statements on the benefits of the nyungne practice that were made by the Bodhisattva Chenrezig himself. Most of these statements include assurances such as, "This is so certain that if this does not happen, may I never attain buddhahood," and so forth. The first source of these is a text called *The Unstoppable Dharani of the Thousand-Armed and Thousand-Eyed Chenrezig*. In this text Chenrezig is addressing the Buddha and says, "Bhagavat, if any sentient being recites this mantra of myself, the Great Compassionate One, and retains it *[which means to recite it regularly]*, having done so, if they then are reborn in any of the three lower states then may I never attain perfect awakening." Elsewhere in the same text he says, "If someone, no matter who they are, recites this mantra and is not reborn in a buddha realm, then may I never attain perfect awakening."

He continues, "If someone who recites this does not achieve all of their wishes in this life, then stop calling this mantra 'the dharani of great compassion.' However, this does not include those who perform the practice with an unvirtuous motivation or whose minds are not one-pointedly focused." He also says, "And further, if during the practice a single thought of doubt about the practice's efficacy is generated, then there is no doubt that the result that you are trying to achieve will not be achieved." Then he says:

> If a sentient being embezzles the provisions or possessions of the sangha or wastes them, even if a thousand buddhas were to appear in the world before them and they were to confess what they had done in the presence of those thousand buddhas, those actions would not be purified. Nevertheless, if such a person simply recited this mantra of great compassion they could be fully purified. If someone were to steal the provisions and possessions of the Three Jewels or waste them, even if all the buddhas of the ten directions appeared before them and they confessed what they had done in their presence, those actions could not be purified. However, if they recite this dharani of great compassion, then they actually can purify it because in effect by reciting it their confession is heard by all buddhas of the ten directions. Anyone who engages in the ten unvirtuous actions, the five acts of immediate consequence, who denigrates other beings, who disrupts or destroys other people's opportunity for renewal and purification, who destroys the moral discipline of others, destroys stupas or temples, steals the possessions of the sangha, and destroys the discipline of celibacy of others, even such intense wrongdoing as these will be

completely purified by this practice. There is no basis whatsoever for doubt about the efficacy of this practice of mantra. However, if someone generates the slightest doubt about it, then it will not purify even the slightest wrongdoing, never mind serious wrongdoing. If someone recites it with some degree of doubt, while it will not totally purify any wrongdoing, it will nevertheless establish an indirect cause for the future attainment of awakening.

In another text he says:

I will lead all of these beings imprisoned in samsara to unsurpassable awakening. I will accomplish the activity of emptying samsara from its depths. With my eleven faces I continually gaze upon sentient beings and with my thousand arms I continually stroke them. If a child of good family, when their previous aspirations for Dharma have ripened, abides in the fast for two days, or even for one day, and calls me by name one hundred and eight times, pays homage and thinks of me, then even if that being has previously committed the five actions of immediate consequence, they will be definitely led to the realm of Sukhavati and will be born there. If someone thinks of me, then even if that person had previously engaged in the five actions of immediate consequence, simply by keeping me in mind they will be led to and will be reborn in the realm of Sukhavati. There is no possibility that such a person, regardless of what they had done, could be reborn in lower states. If such a person were to be reborn, after having thought of me, in lower states, then I will never attain unsurpassable awakening.

Chenrezig expressed this type of commitment in many sutras and tantras. One of the abilities of a bodhisattva is that their aspirations or their promises are always accomplished. They have the power of speech that ensures the accomplishment of their aspirations, which is among the ten powers of a bodhisattva on the higher levels. Having that power, even if the nature of space itself were to change, there could not occur any change in the efficacy of these aspirations of the Bodhisattva Chenrezig.

The Benefits of Reciting or Recollecting the Name of Chenrezig

The second point is a description of the benefits of reciting or recollecting the name of Chenrezig. Because Chenrezig is the embodiment of the compassion of all buddhas, in a sense he is more effective in enacting compassion than all buddhas. In *The Dharani of the Eleven-Faced Chenrezig* it says:

> If someone were to recite and constantly recollect the names of millions or billions of buddhas, and someone else were to for a moment recollect my name, then the value of these two recollections would be equal. Anyone who calls me by name will attain a state beyond reversal. They will be freed from illness, from obscuration, and from all danger. All of their wrongdoing of body, speech, and mind will melt away and be purified. Anyone who undertakes or recollects or reads or recites or teaches this mantra that I have taught will receive these benefits, so what need is there to say that anyone who practices it intensively will receive these benefits? Those who practice it will discover unsurpassable awakening as though it had been placed in the palm of their hand. They will imbibe it, they will realize it, and they will achieve all of its excellence.

In that way it was emphasized by Chenrezig himself that he embodies great blessings, especially for beings in the age of degeneration and in particular for disciples of this tradition.

When Chenrezig first generated bodhicitta, he made the aspiration that in the future when beings had developed the coarsest mental afflictions and were engaging in extensive and seriously negative actions, he would be available to liberate them. In particular, this aspiration applies to those who are earnestly engaged in the ten unvirtuous actions, in the five actions of immediate consequence, in the denigration of the holy and of the Dharma, in the destruction of stupas and of temples, in the violation of moral commitments, in the embezzlement or theft of the belongings of the Three Jewels, in the destruction of sanghas of the celibate, and in the performance of wrongdoing such as fishing, hunting, and butchery. He aspired that all beings in the age of degeneration who engage in unvirtuous actions could be liberated simply by calling Chenrezig by name and reciting his mantra. He aspired that he would be supreme in liberating such beings, that he would be their protector and guardian, and that he would be their assistant and rescuer.

While there are innumerable forms of Chenrezig, the root of all the other forms — the actual source of emanation — is considered to be the form with eleven faces, one thousand arms, and one thousand eyes. In particular, this form of Chenrezig is the most intimately connected with his commitment to benefit beings in the age of degeneration. Therefore, it has been taught by the gurus of this lineage that because of the intimate connection between this form of the deity and his aspiration to benefit beings in the age of degeneration, meditation on this form has extraordinary blessing under the present circumstances.

In the old liturgies of the nyungne practice we also find the statement, "In the future, in order to be of benefit to beings, to bring them happiness and to bring them peace, may I have one thousand arms and may each of the hands on those arms bear an eye." Therefore, as soon as he made that aspiration he came to possess one thousand arms and one thousand eyes. He was empowered by all buddhas, and it is taught that at that time eighteen signs occurred which auspiciously indicated his future ability to liberate beings.

In one of the most important tantras connected with all forms of Chenrezig practice, the *Lotus Net Tantra* (*Pema Drawa* in Tibetan), it says:

> In the future, a guide of beings called Shakya will appear in the realm of tolerance. *["Tolerance" is a reference to our particular galaxy.]* Among the many habitations of humans within that realm there will be a land of pretas. *[As you know, "preta" normally refers to hungry ghosts, but in a footnote in our text it says that this is understood as a reference to the Bön tradition of animal sacrifice.]* Therefore in the midst of such darkness, in order to benefit beings and the teachings, like a flash of lightning in the midst of the grimmest darkness, I will appear as the holder of awareness mantra with eleven faces and a thousand arms and a thousand eyes with a body bearing these characteristics. At that time some people with good fortune will call me by name and will feel devotion for this form. They will recite this awareness mantra. Any of those who do this will accomplish their wishes in this world and after this life will attain genuine wisdom.

This extract from the *Lotus Net Tantra* is understood to be statements made by the Bodhisattva Chenrezig when in a previous eon he generated bodhicitta in the presence of the Buddha Amitayus. It is understood to contain prophesies both by Amitayus and by Chenrezig himself. Elsewhere in the same tantra it says:

> Better than calling by name and praising as many buddhas as there are grains of sand in a hundred rivers like the Ganges, would it be for a son or daughter of good family *[which means of the mahayana]* to simply call me by name and recollect me and continually recite my awareness mantra. They will quickly attain the state of utter joy. *[The state or level of utter joy refers to the first bodhisattva level.]* They will quickly attain unsurpassable awakening as though they discovered it in the palm of their own hand.

In the *Lotus Sutra* it says:

> If someone were to pay homage to and call by name, venerate, and serve with all sorts of offerings as many buddhas as there are grains of sand in sixty-two rivers like the Ganges, and someone else were to call Chenrezig by name once and pay homage to Chenrezig once, the merit of those two people would be equal.

In *The Box Sutra* it says:

> Child of good family, it is like this. If someone were to offer to as many buddhas as there would be grains of sand in twelve rivers like the Ganges, robes, clothing, bedding, healing medicine, and so forth—all the things that could be desired or needed—the aggregate of merit they would accrue would roughly be equal to the amount of merit in one hair on the body of Chenrezig.

Through such quotations we can infer that the benefits of venerating, praising, and meditating upon the Bodhisattva Chenrezig far exceed those of meditating upon any other deity.

The Vajrayana Aspects of the Benefits

The third point is based on the fact that this is a vajrayana practice based on a mandala of secret mantra. Therefore, it is far more powerful and effective than a practice of the sutras alone. This is so principally because—as is born out in many scriptures concerning the practice of tantra—the practice of vajrayana brings siddhi or attainment much more quickly and much more easily. For example, in the *Tantra of the Lotus Net*, it says:

> Because you achieve your aim through various methods, such as mantra, substances, and mudras, this

vehicle of secret mantra is far superior to other vehicles. It need not be said therefore that the result of its earnest practice is also superior. Simply through holding or retaining mantra and mudra, sickness and disturbances will be dispelled. The obscurations accumulated throughout eons will be purified. In these ways it is superior. Even if you are impoverished or denigrated socially and you enter this vehicle of mantra you will find comfort. Through practicing it even a little bit, a great power will arise in your practice. It is also superior in that way.

The Benefits of the Dharanis

The fourth point focuses on the benefits of the repetition of the dharanis of this practice, the long dharani and the short dharani. The short dharani is the second half of the long dharani and is recited on its own during the nyungne. In *The Lotus Net* it says:

> This dharani is the quintessence of awareness mantras. It embodies the unstoppable power of Eleven-Faced Chenrezig. It is like medicine for beings. It brings them bliss. It dispels all illness. It purifies all wrongdoing. It dispels all bad dreams and inauspicious indications. It averts untimely death and inappropriate states of mind. It pacifies agitation, disputation, maras, obstructers, and demons. It brings about all of your wishes in this world. It imprisons all of the weapons of Mara and all of the obstacles of Mara. It prevents disaster from water and fire, from wind and earth, from earthquakes, from poisons, and from curses, from zombies, thieves, and non-human spirits. You will be protected from all of these things by this awareness mantra. If you are diligent in reciting this, you will be impervious even to harm brought about by the gods. Even if you have strong negative karma from the past, it will be gradually purified and finally completely purified.

Elsewhere in the same tantra it says:

> Someone who pays homage to the Buddha and venerates the buddhas, goes for refuge to them and confesses their wrongdoing, who rejoices in the virtue of others and recites this mantra twenty-one times, will be granted assurance of purification by all buddhas without exception of the ten directions. Even if they have violated the four roots of moral discipline, killing, stealing, adultery, and lying, and even if they have engaged in the five actions of immediate consequence—killing either of their parents or an arhat, causing a schism in the sangha, or drawing blood from the body of a buddha with malicious intent—all of this wrongdoing will be purified.

Elsewhere in the same tantra it says:

> Always arising early in the morning, behaving virtuously in accordance with the Dharma, and reciting this one hundred and eight times, you will attain ten benefits in this very life. You will always be free of sickness. You will be protected by all buddhas and devas. You will acquire wealth, food, jewels, and clothing. Your enemies will be subdued. You will be without fear or danger. You will be respected by your friends of good position. You will be free of harm from poisons, spirits, ghosts, and demons. Your body will smell sweet or fragrant and will be delightful to all. You will be free from those who bear you spite or who speak abusively to you. You will be free from contagious illness, free from untimely death, and you will attain buddhahood. As well, you will attain the following four qualities: (1) at the time of your death you will see the buddhas and light will appear in the sky; (2) you will be venerated by devas and you will never pass to lower states; (3) you will be reborn in Sukhavati; and (4) you will perfect the emulation of the examples of all buddhas and bodhisattvas.

In the *Dharani of the Eleven-Faced Chenrezig* it says:

> Bhagavat, this essence mantra of the Eleven-Faced One was taught by eleven billion buddhas. In that way, it is medicine for the suffering of all beings. It pacifies all of their sickness. It averts all wrongdoing, inauspiciousness, and bad dreams. It averts untimely death. It causes those without faith to generate faith. It pacifies all obstructers and deceivers. Because of these benefits I will explain it. Bhagavat, beings are protected by this essence mantra and they are brought to peace by it. There is nothing in the world—including the realm of the gods—that can prevent this mantra from bringing beings that peace, unless it is the previously accumulated karma of those beings themselves.

Elsewhere in the same text it presents another set of ten benefits:

> If arising early you recite it one hundred and eight times, you will come to possess ten qualities in this life. If you ask what those ten are, they are: (1) that you will not be afflicted by a certain illness. *[This illness mentioned in the text is explained by some as bronchitis, but it is uncertain that it literally means that.]*; (2) you will be cared for by all buddhas; (3) you will acquire wealth and provisions effortlessly; (4) all of your enemies will be subdued; (5) rulers will treat you with affection; (6) you will be unaffected by mineral poison, contagious illnesses, fire, water, untimely death, and so forth. As well, you will come to possess four qualities: *[These are the last four of the list of ten.]* (1) at the time of your death you will see the tathagatas; (2) you will not be reborn in lower states; (3) you will not feel anxiety at the time of your death; and (4) immediately after your death you will be reborn in the realm of Sukhavati.

In the same text it also says:

> By reciting this dharani even once, you purify the four root violations of moral discipline. By reciting it even once, you purify the five actions of immediate consequence. Therefore, what need there be to say that it is worth practicing earnestly in order to achieve all the benefits that I have described? The benefits of it are such that you generate the roots of virtue of billions and billions of buddhas. Therefore, if by reciting it even once such benefits are accrued, what need is there to describe the benefits of continually reciting it and practicing its associated meditation? In short, by doing so you will accomplish completely all of your wishes.

Elsewhere it says:

> If someone on the 14th or 15th day of the lunar month abides in fasting and recites this essence of awareness mantra, having properly taken the eight vows of renewal and purification, and practices properly in accordance with the Dharma and recollects me, Chenrezig, with a one-pointed mind while reciting this awareness mantra, they will shorten samsara by forty thousand eons.

In the *Lotus Net Tantra*, immediately after Chenrezig has taught this particular dharani, it says, "By reciting this essence mantra a thousand times you will acquire whatever siddhis you wish for." In association with the presentation of this root mantra, when describing the way it should be practiced in more detail, he says:

> Merely by reciting this mantra of the protector Avalokiteshvara, for the person who recites it there will not occur the fifteen types of inauspicious death. They will achieve the fifteen types of auspicious rebirth. They will be free from famine, punishment of

tyrants, poison, weapons, warfare, tigers, snakes, and other predatory or carnivorous animals, poisoned food, and death through fire or water. All these things will never endanger them. They will be reborn in a country with religious leaders, a place that is inhabited by bodhisattvas, and which is in a good state. They will encounter spiritual teachers. Their faculties will be complete. They will delight in virtue and will be naturally moral in their behavior. Their associates will be benevolent. They will be wealthy. They will be respected by others and will acquire all they need. They will be happy, and they will be protected by the guardians of the world. They will see the face of the Buddha and will understand or realize the profound meaning. They will be loving toward their inferiors. They will have such compassion that they will cry through the force of it. They will be delighted in the recollection of the qualities. They will have faith in the Three Jewels. Their intelligence will be excellent and it will increase. They will be free from inappropriate mental engagement *[i.e., thoughts]*. They will have faith in the Buddha's teachings and will be reborn again and again in such a situation.

In a tantra called *The Lotus Crown* it says:

> A son or daughter of good family who recites this mantra even once, or recollects it, or keeps it in mind, or wears it on his or her body, even if they have performed the five actions of immediate consequence or those forms of wrongdoing which closely approach those actions, will not be reborn in the hells, as a preta, or as an animal. They will not experience the eight unrestful states. They will not be menaced by predators, rakshasas, non-humans, sickness, or other dangers.

Such statements are set forth in great detail in these texts in general. The various forms of Chenrezig, including the eleven-faced, thousand-armed, thousand-eyed form and the eight-armed form called the King of Space (Namkhay Gyalpo), can vary a little bit in different traditions in their actual appearance such as the colors of the various faces, what is held in their arms and so on, and in the mantras. In the tradition of Lakshmi, the source of the nyungne practice, the principal mantra recited is this dharani of the Eleven-Faced Chenrezig. As has been mentioned, there is the long form of it, which is the whole dharani, and the short form, which is just the second half of it recited alone.

There are other mantras or dharanis taught in the sadhana composed by Nagarjuna. In that tradition there is another dharani called the "dharani of the blue-necked one." The summary of its benefits, which comes from the tradition of Arya Nagarjuna and Arya Deva, is as follows:

> By reciting this dharani even once, even if the four root downfalls of moral discipline have occurred, they will be completely purified. By recollecting this dharani, you will be continually regarded with compassion by the thousand-armed form of Chenrezig. You will be protected by his thousand hands. Even if you have engaged in the five actions of immediate consequence, the five actions which are close to them, or have taken the wealth of the sangha and so forth, by reciting this dharani even once, all of that will be purified and exhausted. However, all of this is only true if you have no doubt. You will not experience the twenty-five types of inauspicious death. You will achieve the fifteen types of auspicious birth. Anyone who hears the name of the deity as present in this essence mantra will purify all of the wrongdoing—even the heavy wrongdoing—they have engaged in during countless lives throughout countless eons. Therefore what need is there to say that those who recite it will be able to purify anything. If you recite it unceasingly, there will be no difficulty in your attainment of the ten bodhisattva bhumis. What need is there to say that you will acquire all mundane merit as well.

Because the benefits are so extensive, it is appropriate to recite this mantra at least a few times. It says in the original tantras (the speaker being Chenrezig himself), "It is appropriate to recite this mantra while recollecting my master Amitabha."

The Benefits of *Om Mani Peme Hung*

Next is the fifth point, which deals with the benefits of reciting the six-syllable mantra *om mani peme hung*.

The mantra *om mani peme hung* is regarded as the quintessence of all forms of Chenrezig. All of the various benefits that are taught to arise from the practices of the various forms of Chenrezig as they are presented in the four tantras (the kriya, charya, yoga, and anuttarayoga tantras) are said to be complete within this six-syllable mantra. Therefore, in the *Lotus Crown Tantra* it says:

> The abbreviated mantra in all of these forms of the deity is *om mani peme hung*. By reciting this you will become the lord of the three families—its benefits are that great. By reciting this mantra you will see both the dharmakaya and the rupakaya or form body aspects of the Great Compassionate One, Chenrezig.

In the *Box Sutra* it says:

> This mantra is the sacred quintessence of the Bodhisattva Chenrezig. Anyone who keeps this mantra of six syllables in mind and recites it, that being will come to possess great merit. While they recite it as many buddhas will assemble around them as there would be grains of sand in ninety-six rivers like the river Ganges. As many bodhisattvas as there are subtle particles in the whole world will assemble around them. They will abide in the gateway to the completion of the six perfections. Virtuous devas of all thirty-two classes will assemble around them.

They will be protected from the four directions by the four great Kings. They will be protected by the monarchs of nagas and by millions of their subjects. They will be protected by all of the yakshas who live throughout the earth. In each of the pores of the skin of someone who recites this mantra ten million buddhas will enter. In each of their lifetimes for several lifetimes after reciting this they will acquire the wish-fulfilling jewel. All of the small beings that live in their bodies *[this refers to beings such as the bacteria in our intestines and so on]* will rejoice in the practice that the person has done. If someone keeps the written form of this mantra on his or her body at all times they will attain the indestructible vajra body and after their death their body will produce miraculous relics. They will attain the wisdom of the Buddha. Whoever recites this mantra will generate inexhaustible confidence, will generate a pure aggregate of wisdom, possess great compassion, and each day will complete the practice of the six perfections. He or she will become a monarch among holders of awareness. They will quickly attain unsurpassable awakening. Everyone that they touch with their hand will become a bodhisattva in their last samsaric life. If they are seen by other beings, even animals, then those beings that see them will be free from the sufferings of birth, aging, sickness, and death, and they too will become bodhisattvas in their last life.

In the same sutra it continues:

It would be possible with the wisdom of a buddha to calculate the number of subtlest particles throughout the universe. It would be possible to calculate the number of grains of sand at the bottom of an ocean, the number of drops of water in this world, the number of kernels of grain, the number of leaves found in this world, or the number of drops of water that fall throughout this world in a twelve-year period. All of these things could be counted by one possessing a buddha's wisdom. However, the merit accumulated by saying the six-syllable mantra even once could never be calculated.

It is taught that to recite the six-syllable mantra even once is more meritorious than to establish all beings throughout the entire world at the seventh bodhisattva level. Anyone who enters into the practice of the recitation of the six-syllable mantra has entered into the practice of all eighty-four thousand collections of Dharma. If someone were to offer gold and jewels each day to as many buddhas as there are subtle particles throughout the universe, the karmic result of that would be equal to the karmic result of reciting the six-syllable mantra even once. In short, its qualities are inconceivable. If you recite it, you will acquire one hundred and eight types of meditative absorption. By comparison, all other forms of yoga or practice are like a husk and this is like the kernel or the essence. In that way, through the many sutras and tantras, this mantra is highly praised.

Most of the quotations from the sutras and tantras about this mantra were collected and are found in the collected works of King Songtsen Gampo. Throughout Songtsen Gampo's writings, all of the cycles of practice he presented are centered entirely upon the repetition of the six-syllable mantra. In short, there is no mantra that can be recited or said that has the same benefits and the same qualities as the six-syllable mantra *om mani peme hung*. It is therefore appropriate to continually recite it.

The Benefits of Some Additional Dharanis

The sixth point is an explanation of the benefits of some other dharanis included in the text, ones that were added by the gurus of the lineage. These dharanis are not actually in the form of the nyungne that is done nowadays in the Karma Kagyu tradition, which is a fairly concise one. If you do not recognize the names of these mantras, that may be why. The first of these is called "The Dharani of the Wish-Fulfilling Jewel" and it has some variations. The form of the deity can vary and the actual words of the mantra can vary as well. Its benefits are explained in the text called *The Dharani of the Wish-Fulfilling Jewel,* which says:

> If a son or daughter of good family, of any of the four types of the Buddha's retinue, wishes to immediately achieve the final fruition of the path, they should exert themselves in the practice of this wish-fulfilling jewel. In the context of such a practice, do not pay any attention to astrological conjunctions. Do not engage in the practice of fasting. Do not worry about washing or putting on clean clothing.

This quote requires some explanation. As with some previous quotes, a "son or daughter of good family" means someone who has generated bodhicitta. "The four types of the buddha's retinue" means a lay disciple, a novice monastic, someone with intermediate monastic ordination, or a fully ordained monastic.

Then it says not to worry about whether it is an auspicious or inauspicious day based on the lunar calendar or the movements of constellations, or engage in fasting, putting on clean clothes, and washing. In general, of course, when you do nyungne practice that is exactly what you do. What is being taught about this particular mantra is that it does not depend upon such conditions and therefore can be practiced outside of them and you will still receive its benefits.

In the same way, there is also no liturgy of practice needed. With almost all mantras, when you recite the mantra you have to do it in the context of some kind of liturgical practice. It can be brief or it can be long, but the benefits of the mantra are said to be limited in that type of context. However, with the mantras of the Bodhisattva Chenrezig such as *om mani peme hung,* they can be chanted at any time under any circumstances whether or not it is within a formal liturgical practice, and it will still bring benefit. The text continues:

Rest for the Fortunate

> The benefits of the mantra are accomplished simply by reciting it or reading it. Therefore, have no doubt about the benefit of its recitation. There is no other mantra that is equal to this in power. Your previous wrongdoing and obscuration will be exhausted simply by reciting it. You will not be reborn in the realm of uninterrupted torment and your wrongdoing will be purified before your death.

The same text continues:

> The wrongdoing of such actions as the five actions of immediate consequence will be completely purified. Therefore, sickness and contagion and curses that are the actions of malevolent spirits such as yakshas and rakshasas will not affect you. Poison and weapons and fire and water will not affect you. Thieves and tyrants and enemies and untimely death will not endanger you. You will not have bad dreams. You will be victorious over all disputation. By reciting it one hundred and eight times, on that day you will see the Bodhisattva Chenrezig, and will receive assurance from him and attainment. All buddhas such as Amitabha and their realms, such as Sukhavati and the Potala and so forth, will be seen by you. At the time of your death, you will see the Bodhisattva Chenrezig and will be born in a buddha realm instantaneously from a lotus flower. Throughout all your lives you will remember your previous lives. You will never be reborn in lower states, and you will attain buddhahood.

Another dharani that is included in the elaborate forms of the nyungne practice is one called "The Dharani of the Ten Levels." There are ten variations on this dharani, each one corresponding to one of the ten bodhisattva levels. By reciting these, you will accomplish the qualities of those ten levels. These dharanis come from *The Examination of Amoghapasha*, which is the name of one of the kriya tantras.

Another dharani often used is one that people may be more familiar with, because in the Buddhist tradition you often find it above doors. It is called the "Lotus Crown Protuberance Mantra." Briefly stated, the benefits of this ten-syllable mantra are that anyone who recites it one hundred thousand times will abide in the ten bodhisattva levels, and will attain the irreversible state of that deity, the Lotus Crown Protuberance. By reciting it even once, you will accomplish the activity of a buddha. Therefore what need is there to say that if you recite it with exertion you will accomplish a great deal? Reciting it in the context of one day's fasting, or in fact even recollecting this mantra for a moment, will purify all of your previous wrongdoing such as the five actions of immediate consequence that would otherwise cause you to be born immediately after your death in the realm of uninterrupted torment. Those who recite it will never be reborn again in a lower state, and in future lives they will achieve birth for the duration of an eon as world rulers in the realm of Abhirati ("the joyous") and in the realm of Sukhavati. In that way, they will always be happy. If you recite this ten-syllable mantra ten times a day focused on the benefit of other beings, you will generate the roots of virtue of as many buddhas as there are grains of sand in the river Ganges. Immediately after your death you will be reborn in Sukhavati, and you will attain hundreds of samadhis.

If you blow on clean sand when reciting the mantra and then scatter the sand on the bodies of people or animals that have passed away, or on their bones or in cemeteries or charnel grounds, then all of those beings — even if they have violated moral discipline and had other faults — will not be reborn in lower states and they will immediately be reborn in a higher realm. If you write it on birch bark and place it inside a stupa or a monument, then all the humans and animals who walk under the shadow of that monument will be reborn in higher states. If you recite the mantra and blow upon a conch, consecrating the conch shell with it, then all who hear the sound of that conch will attain a state of irreversibility and rebirth in Sukhavati. Anyone who hears this mantra will be reborn in a higher realm. If you use the mantra to consecrate sandalwood powder and then you burn the sandalwood powder in a sangha dwelling such as a monastery, then all who smell the scent of that incense will achieve the state of perfect awakening. If you fumigate your robes with that incense and then put them on, your wrongdoing and obscurations will be purified. If you burn it at a crossroads, then all disputation and contagion in that region will end. If you burn it in the wild, then that place will be free from warfare, thievery, and predators. If you burn it where there is an epidemic, it will be pacified.

The next mantra that is discussed is the "Dharani of Endless Gates." This dharani is used in the nyungne practice that we do. Someone who recites it will be thought of by all buddhas, and maras will never be able to disturb them. Their karmic obscurations will be quickly purified, and they will attain boundless confidence. This mantra has a particular function of purifying or removing the obscurations that prevent you from seeing the face of the deity, from having a vision of the deity, and from hearing the deity's speech.

To sum up, someone who assiduously performs the practice of Chenrezig and recites the requisite number of the various mantras is beneficial to everyone around them. Everyone who sees, hears, recollects, or touches the person will have the seed of liberation planted within them. In *The Collection of the Sutras* it says:

> For example, if someone who regularly recites this mantra of the Great Compassionate One bathes or washes in a river or an ocean, then all of the beings that inhabit that river or ocean and all of the beings who have any contact with the water of that river or that ocean will be benefited. Their karma, including even their most serious wrongdoing, will be purified and in future lives they will be reborn from a lotus flower in the realm of Sukhavati. Therefore, what need is there to say that those who actually practice

it themselves will derive great benefit. When you are traveling, the wind that touches the body of the practitioner of this mantra and then touches any other person will cause those other people to be purified. Even their greatest wrongdoing and obscuration will be purified. They will not be reborn in lower states. They will be reborn in the presence of the buddhas. In short, know the benefits of the recitation of these mantras to be inestimable and immeasurable.

Concerning this, the Bodhisattva Dawa Gyaltsen, the first Tibetan member of the lineage of the nyungne practice, said, "If these mantras and dharanis are heard by animals just before or after their death it will cause them to achieve precious human existence and will place the seed of bodhicitta within them such that eventually they too will be reborn in Sukhavati." This is particularly significant in this country where you normally have so many animals surrounding you, including pets and domestic animals. By reciting such mantras in the hearing of an animal regularly — and especially when it dies — you can actually bring tremendous benefit.

The Benefits of the Practice Ritual

The seventh point concerns the benefit that comes from doing the practice ritual of the nyungne. In the *Lotus Net Tantra* it says:

> Take the vows of renewal and purification in the presence of an image of the deity on the fourteenth, fifteenth, and especially the eighth day of the lunar month. The image should be made of stainless white sandalwood and so forth *[which means a wood that is not poisonous]*. It can also be made of clay, stone, or precious metals. In one of these materials, construct an image of the sugata. It may also be painted. Having created an image of either the single principal deity or of all of the deities of the mandala, and think-

ing that they are all present, you will quickly actually see them.

Elsewhere in the same tantra it says, "With a vase that has all of the proper qualities and with water, by consecrating these with mantra there is no doubt that all of your wishes will be accomplished." This refers to the use of the vase in the nyungne practice, in which case the vase has to have a certain shape and the water within it has to contain the twenty-five different substances such as powder of jewels, medicinal powders, and so on. In an old form of the nyungne liturgy it says:

> Anyone who practices this mantra should take the eight vows on the full moon day of the month. Dressing in clean clothing in the presence of a properly consecrated stupa which contains relics or an image of the Buddha, construct the mandala with the powder of white sandalwood and place various flowers upon it, fumigate it with incense and light lamps, and generate devotion for the Buddha. If having done that you recite this mantra one hundred and eight times, the Bodhisattva Chenrezig will actually be present in that mandala and whatever karmic obscurations you possess, such as those caused by the five actions of immediate consequence and others, will all be purified. All of your previous actions of body, speech, and mind will be purified. You will receive the great empowerment of rays of light from all buddhas. You will complete the ten levels of the practice of the six perfections: generosity, patience, moral discipline, diligence, meditation, and discernment.

This quotation is from the *Lotus Net Tantra,* and because, like the nyungne practice, this text is a kriya tantra of the lotus family, it is considered to apply to the nyungne practice.

The text called *The Unstoppable Dharani* says:

> If someone continually offers a handful of incense or flowers to an image of this deity and recites the dharani, then they will generate a tremendous compassion that embodies all of the qualities of the world. Finally, they will manifestly accomplish the great power to practically benefit beings.

Another statement from the *Lotus Net Tantra* is:

> If you recite this mantra over medicine that is to be given for appropriate ailments *(that is, ailments that you would normally treat with those particular medicines)*, whether the medicine is to be eaten or to be applied externally, or even used as fumigation, the medicine will certainly be effective. If you recite it over thread *(this refers to the thread that is used to make protection knots or cords worn around the neck)* or clothing, then in the same way they will dispel all harm.

In the text called *The Dharani of the Eleven-Faced Chenrezig* it says, "If you recite the dharani one hundred and eight times over water and that water is sprinkled on your body, it will dispel all obscurations and obstructers. All of your wishes will be accomplished."

It was said by the Bodhisattva Dawa Gyaltsen, "If someone does this nyungne practice even once they will be reborn in Sukhavati. They will turn their back on samsara and will attain the qualities of the first bhumi." On the first day of the nyungne, which is called the preliminary day, you eat one meal, and on the second day you do not eat or drink anything. If you offer the food for that one meal to even one person doing the practice, that is of the same merit as offering food to a bodhisattva of the eighth level. On the morning of the third day a kind of gruel is served. If you make and serve that porridge to even one of the participants of the nyungne, that is like serving it to five hundred pratyekabuddhas.

If you serve food to someone who is doing a nyinay, that is equal to serving food to an arhat. Someone who offers food to people who are doing a nyungne will not be reborn in lower states, will never suffer from sickness, violence, or famine in future lives. Throughout their future lives they will be happy and prosperous, and they will have generated bodhicitta which they will continue to develop throughout all future lives.

However, this section concludes, "For any and all of these benefits to be accrued what is of the greatest importance is having confidence and freedom from doubt about this. If you have the slightest doubt about the benefit of the virtuous action or practice it will not lead to any benefit whatsoever." This was made clear in earlier parts of the text when quotations from various parts of the tantras were given, showing how in any deity or mantra practice, the most important thing is lack of doubt.

The Benefits of the Generation and Completion Stages

The eighth point describes the general benefits of the meditation on the generation and completion stages, and the particular benefits when it is practiced in the nyungne.

When the benefits of the six perfections are presented, it is always taught that each one has a greater benefit or power than the one that preceded it. For example, moral discipline brings more benefit than generosity, patience more benefit than morality, diligence more than patience, meditation more than diligence, and prajna or discernment brings the greatest benefit of all. Therefore, the benefit of the cultivation of discernment—especially in the sense of meditation on emptiness—is supreme. In the *Samadhiraja Sutra* it says, "It is of more merit to take seven steps toward a place of solitude in order to meditate on selflessness there than it would be to establish all sentient beings of the three realms on the path of the ten virtues." The three realms are the desire realm, the form realm, and the realm of formlessness. What is being stated here is that even intending to meditate upon emptiness is more powerful than any act of conventional virtue.

In the same vein, the *Sutra that Describes Suchness* says, "Shariputra, it is of much more merit to remain in even placement in meditation on suchness, the nature of all things, for the duration of a fingersnap than it would be to study for the duration of an eon." In *The Great Realization* it says, "It is of more use to meditate for one session than to save the lives of all sentient beings of the three realms." Thus, the benefits of meditation on emptiness are inconceivable and, ultimately, indescribable.

However, even greater than that is the benefit of this type of meditation done in the context of vajrayana or mantra practice. Even a small act of virtue becomes tremendously powerful if it is done in that context. Therefore, in the root tantra of Kalachakra it says, "If people such as hunters and woodcutters and those who have committed the five actions of immediate consequence engage in this practice of mantra, they will attain buddhahood in this very life." Hunters are mentioned here because of their accumulation of wrongdoing in general. The reference to woodcutters is more of a cultural one. In the caste system which existed in India, such individuals would conventionally be considered unlikely to be able to accomplish anything of a spiritual nature. The reference to the five actions of immediate consequence is a clear description of those things that are the worst possible actions that anyone could do. Therefore, it is said that by practicing vajrayana even such individuals can attain buddhahood in one lifetime.

Even an act of virtue that we would normally consider to be a conceptual act of virtue and therefore somehow defiled, can become tremendously powerful and a source of great merit if it is performed in connection with the practice of mantra. For example, it is taught that it is of more merit to sponsor the creation of one image of a deity or a buddha as described in the tantras than it would be to create one hundred images as described in the sutras. Furthermore, the actual practice of meditation of the generation and completion stages with their complete characteristics and with the proper motivation is much greater than that, and therefore cannot even be described. It is definitely the case that such practices will quickly purify all obscurations, both karma and kleshas, and quickly lead to the attainment of both supreme and common attainments. "Supreme attainment" means spiritual awakening, and "common attainment" refers to all manner of well-being. These attainments will be achieved in this life, or in the bardo after this life.

By doing the practice of the generation and completion stages, you will immediately find that your body becomes well and comfortable. Your speech becomes powerful and your mind becomes filled with the wisdom of realization. At your death, there will be auspicious signs such as rainbows and relics appearing from your body, and earthquakes will occur. Among all the different vajrayana practices that there are, this particular deity, the Eleven-Faced Chenrezig, is especially considered to be the essence of all buddhas. Therefore, by meditating upon this single deity you are meditating simultaneously upon the mandalas of all buddhas. For example, the four colors of his various faces embody the four activities. By meditating upon him in that form, you therefore will accomplish these activities effortlessly. Another example is that it is taught that a particular benefit will arise from the visualization of each of his different hands.

All of this concerns the benefit of doing the nyungne practice, including the recitation of its mantra, as it is actually taught in the original scriptural source of this practice. However, if in addition to this it is done in the manner of an elaborate practice with offerings and so forth as is the custom according to the instructions of the gurus of this lineage, then there are even greater benefits. In a similar way, each of the parts of the seven-branch prayer that is included in this practice has its own particular and inconceivably great benefits.

The Commitments of the Nyungne Practice

The fifth topic is concerned not only with commitments to be kept during the nyungne itself, but also with the general commitments for someone who takes the nyungne as their principal practice.

An important point to understand is that the very life force of tantric practice is samaya (commitment). This means that if you do not maintain the samayas required by your specific practice, then not only will the practice not work, but all sorts of things will go wrong, both in this life and in future lives. On the other hand, if you keep the samayas of the practice then the exact opposite will occur. You will quickly attain supreme attainment.

The particular samayas in this context would apply to someone who has taken the vow of refuge and the bodhisattva vow, and has taken a kriya tantra empowerment introducing them to the mandala of one of the buddha families, which in the case of the nyungne would be the padma (lotus) family.

According to the kriya tantras, the samayas that must be kept in general are listed in a kriya tantra called the *Tantra of General Secrets*. Keeping samaya entails avoiding a set of fourteen root downfalls. These are not the same as the fourteen root downfalls in the higher tantras; it is the same number, but it is a very different list. There are also other samayas of kriya tantra that are taught in *The Excellent Accomplishment* and there are five samayas taught in *The Root Tantra of Manjushri*. At this point, however, the writer of our commentary, the Ninth Situ Rinpoche, says "I don't have time to go through these, so you will have to learn them somewhere else." Nevertheless, they are very important.

What he does go through, and which is therefore by implication of greater importance, are the specific samayas of Chenrezig practice. These are the commitments you must follow if you take Chenrezig as your principal deity. These are not merely rules; these are the essence of the practice itself. Therefore they are like the quintessence of the oral instructions of the great Bodhisattva Dawa Gyaltsen.

The first of these is that even if you are denigrated, criticized, reviled, beaten, or harmed in some way without any kind of justification, without your having done anything wrong, you should never be vengeful or try to take revenge. Thus the basic quality of the samayas of Chenrezig practice is that you have the well-known four characteristics of a holy person (i.e., that you do not respond to abuse with abuse, and so forth). Even if someone hits you or steals your belongings or verbally abuses you or speaks harshly of you behind your back, or has terrible attitudes toward you, is jealous of you, is spiteful and so on—no matter what they do, what they say, and what they appear to be thinking, you need to regard it all as the display of the blessing of Chenrezig's body, speech, and mind, and also as the means of purification of your own previous wrongdoing.

In short, whatever happens, whether you are happy or miserable, you need to completely entrust yourself without reservation to Chenrezig, and in that context always think of the bodies of yourself and all other beings as the body of Chenrezig, of their speech as the six-syllable mantra *om mani peme hung,* and of their mind as the unity of the nonconceptual realization of emptiness and compassion. You need to respond to abuse with kindness. Those are the commitments. If you do not have that kind of attitude and that kind of perception of purity, you are contravening the samayas of body, speech, and mind of the Chenrezig practice, by which you cut yourself off from the blessings of the practice and the deity.

It is especially important to always have the attitude that you are ready to and wish to take on the sufferings of others and give all of your virtue and all of your happiness to others. It is within the intention or motivation of bodhicitta that you wish to bring all beings to a state of perfect awakening through your efforts alone.

If this is your main practice, you would do one session of the generation stage of the practice of Chenrezig every day. You would recite the long dharani one hundred times, or at least twenty-one times, or at a minimum fifteen times. In post-meditation, you would try to bring whatever state of mind you have attained in practice into all of your daily activities with mindfulness. In short, use every situation to accumulate virtue, and to accumulate both merit and wisdom.

Part Three: "An Important Digression"

Next we come to the third and final part of the text. It is called an "important digression." This means that it is about important matters, but ones that do not, strictly speaking, pertain only to the practice of nyungne.

The fact that we are still in cyclic existence — and especially that we are still in cyclic existence in these times of degeneration — means that we have not been successfully gotten hold of by any of the buddhas of the past, at least not to the point where we are out of samsara. Therefore, it was in order to bring beings like ourselves to liberation that Buddha Shakyamuni appeared in this world. Buddha Shakyamuni went through great personal sacrifice in order to be able to do this for us. Throughout innumerable eons he gave away his body, his life, and all of his possessions again and again, simply to hear four words of Dharma. He did so in order to gradually complete the path and become a buddha who would benefit beings in a time of degeneracy.

If the Buddha went through great austerity for such a long time just to hear even four words of Dharma, what about us? If we — for whose benefit he did that and for whose benefit he taught what he did — do not make use of the teachings he gave, if we waste what we have received (and needless to say, we have access to more than four words of Dharma), then we are rendering what the Buddha did meaningless and pointless, at least for ourselves. We are not repaying his kindness.

Therefore, the first thing that needs to be understood is that even teaching and listening to Dharma is of great benefit. For example, in the *Sutra of Jampa Sangye* it says:

If you filled as many worlds as there are grains of sand in the river Ganges with gold and gave them all away, that would still be of less benefit than teaching one stanza or one line of Dharma in the age of degeneracy.

In the *Sutra of Dense Ornamentation* it says:

Manjushri, wherever someone is teaching the Dharma or a teacher of Dharma is seen, even the worst wrongdoing is purified. Veneration of them will also purify this wrongdoing.

Elsewhere in the same sutra it says:

By hearing the Dharma you close the gate to a lower rebirth and you plant the seed of nirvana. Once you have heard it, from that time onward you will continue to be reborn as someone with the intelligence and opportunity to gain access to Dharma.

In another sutra it says, "Someone who donates even one of their hairs for the sake of my doctrine will for eighty thousand eons be wealthy." Thus the sponsoring of teachings and so forth is tremendously beneficial. However, as was mentioned earlier in the text, each of the perfections surpasses the benefit of the preceding one, so as beneficial as generosity is, moral discipline is even more beneficial. In the sutra called *The Sage and the Fool* it says:

The merit of monastic ordination is tremendous. Not only that, but the merit of giving someone who is dependent on you for such permission the permission to seek it (such as a son or daughter or an employee), is also tremendous. The merit of generosity has limits, but the merit of monastic ordination in the teachings of the Buddha or in the doctrine of the Buddha is inconceivable. Its merit will never be exhausted until the attainment of nirvana. As well, the benefits of keeping moral discipline once you have taken ordination are indescribable. Even within that, the merit nowadays of taking even one vow for one day is greater than the merit of taking full monastic ordination and keeping it for many years at the time of the Buddha. The merit of pacifying one mental affliction nowadays is greater than the merit of pacifying them all at the time of the Buddha.

Therefore, in the *Samadhiraja Sutra* it says:

> If someone motivated by faith were to donate food and drink, parasols and banners, lamps, garlands, and other things in service of billions of buddhas for as many eons as there are grains of sand in the river Ganges, there would be great merit. But there would be even greater merit if someone at the time of the destruction of Dharma and close to the end of the Buddha's teaching were to maintain for one day and one night one vow of moral discipline.

In spite of those benefits, nowadays most monastics do not keep their vows properly and fall into lower rebirths. On the other hand, most householders, because they still have faith in the sangha, are reborn in the higher realms. This is taught in the *Lotus Sutra*, where it says:

> Ananda, those householders when they die, most of them will be reborn in the heaven called Tushita or Joyous. But the monastics, most of those will fall down. If you ask why that is so, it is because they did not abide within the stricture of their vows. Therefore, in order not to become someone who would be governed by this prediction, it is extremely important to maintain your enthusiasm, diligence, and care or circumspection.

In the same sutra it says:

> Anyone who takes monastic ordination at the time of the exhaustion of my teachings, all of those will attain perfect nirvana in this very fortunate eon.

Since the aspirations and predictions of the Buddha are inconceivably powerful and infallible, it is obvious that making any kind of connection with this type of moral discipline, including the practice of nyungne, has all of these benefits. Therefore having entered this doctrine, keeping these vows for even one day has tremendous benefit.

Furthermore, acts of virtue that are done in connection with an inconceivable object have inconceivable power. For example, it is said that even if someone has committed the five actions of immediate consequence, if they subsequently acquire faith in the Buddha and cause an image of the Buddha to be created, what would otherwise have been a long experience of hell is reduced to a very short one, and they will come to attain thorough transcendence of cyclic existence in the manner of whatever vehicle they have entered.

In another scripture it is said:

> If with a pure motivation you create an image, at best out of precious materials or at least out of clay or scratched with your nail on the side of a wall, the benefits are equal.

And in the *Lotus Sutra* it says:

> When children delighting in play make an image of the Buddha or make a stupa out of sand they have unwittingly caused their own future awakening.

Elsewhere in the same sutra it says:

> If someone makes an image of the Buddha out of lead or iron or earth, even if it is done as play or in secret—even merely by scratching the design of the Buddha's form on a wall idly with his or her nail—everyone who does that will attain awakening. Everyone who does that will become compassionate. Everyone who does such things will be able to liberate millions of beings.

Two sutras called *The Excellent* and *The Piled Mansion* both say the following:

> Greater than offering these billion worlds filled with the seven precious materials to all the shravakas and pratyekabuddhas of the four directions is to offer the central column or life tree to a stupa the size of a *churura*. [*A churura is a little medicinal fruit about the size of an olive.*] In the same way, to place a relic the size of a mustard seed in a statue the size of a barley grain would be of more merit as well.

This text contains many statements and quotations similar to this. It continues:

> If someone were to make a stupa enshrining the relics of the Buddha after he had passed into nirvana, and the stupa were made of the seven precious materials; and, in fact, if you were to make a billion billion times the number of grains of sand in the river Ganges of these, and were to offer flowers, incense, medicinal ointments, and so forth to all of these—in short, if you were to offer whatever you can think of—greater than that would be the merit of writing or creating and venerating one volume or one book of the Buddha's teachings.

Elsewhere in the same sutra it says:

> Of more merit than establishing as many beings in a state of arhatship as there are in as many worlds as there are grains of sand in the river Ganges, would be the merit of sponsoring the writing or actually writing a volume of the prajnaparamita.

Things like prayer flags, mani wheels, mani stones, and so forth are also included in this according to our text. Not only is creating such things of great merit, but making offerings to them, praising them, and having respect for them are tremendously beneficial as well.

In *The Lotus Sutra* it says:

> If someone were to clap a pair of cymbals together once as an offering of sound to a stupa, or offer one flower, or look upon an image of the Buddha painted on a wall even with anger or with agitation, all of these beings will eventually see ten million buddhas as a result. If someone were to for an instant join their palms in devotion for a stupa or slightly bow their head in respect or say "Homage to the Buddha" even while distracted, all of such individuals will eventually accomplish perfect awakening.

The Lotus Sutra contains many similar statements. For example:

> Not only someone who venerates a stupa thinking of me *[the Buddha is speaking here]*, but even someone who casts a single flower into the sky thinking of the Buddha, I say that the result of their virtue will be the attainment of nirvana. If a being who does not have the good fortune to attain nirvana, while thinking of the Buddha casts one flower into the sky, and even if an animal thinks of the Buddha or recollects the Buddha for a second, these things become causes

of awakening. Whenever someone cries because of thinking about the Dharma, or the little hairs on their body stand up, or they sigh with devotion for it—through doing that they will never be reborn as animals. They will never see the realm of Yama and they will never fall into a perverted state. If those born in border regions who therefore have no faith in Dharma see images of the Buddha or stupas and feel some appreciation or liking for these things, that will cause their future awakening.

In particular it says that, "When you do prostrations you will be reborn as a chakravartin as many times as there are particles beneath your body when you do the prostration, and finally you will attain nirvana." Circumambulation produces similar benefits. In *The Sutra of Avalokiteshvara* it says:

> Anyone who circumambulates a stupa commemorating Avalokiteshvara or praises it, their merit will not be exhausted in a million eons. Even greater than venerating billions of buddhas for millions of eons in fortunate times would be one prostration to a stupa in this eon of intolerable misery.

Concerning the benefits of offering butter lamps, the same sutra says:

> A buddha could estimate the number of mustard seeds that would be contained in a treasury the size of billions of buddha realms. But while they could count that, they could not count or estimate the merit of offering one butter lamp to the buddhas.

In *The Sutra on the Offering of Butter Lamps* it says:

> If you so much as illuminate one step on the body of a stupa with a butter lamp that has the power to illuminate like that of a firefly, you will achieve the perfect or complete aggregate of wisdom and will achieve buddhahood.

The Explanation of Acts says:

> Joining your palms in devotion to an image of the Three Jewels, prostrating to it, cleaning it, offering flowers, incense, butter lamps, scented water, fabric, music, and so forth—each of these produces ten benefits both immediate and ultimate.

The Ratnavala Sutra says:

> Someone who praises the Buddha will at the time of their death be under the Buddha's protection and will see his form. Furthermore, to make offerings to an actual buddha who is physically present, and to an image of the buddha or to a stupa that commemorates that buddha while thinking of the buddha—these two are identical in merit.

Both *The Sutra of Piled Flowers* as well as the *Mahaparinirvana Sutra* have this quotation:

> Nanda, it makes no difference whether the Buddha is physically present or has passed into nirvana. Anyone who pays homage with an attitude of faith and venerates the Buddha, the merit of one person doing that in the physical presence of the Buddha and another person doing it in recollection of the Buddha—the merit of these two will be the same.

The Sutra of the Heap of Jewels says:

> If all of the beings of these billion worlds became chakravartins and each of them offered a butter lamp of which the bowl of butter was the size of an ocean and the wick was the size of Mt. Meru, the merit accumulated by all of these would be less than the merit accumulated by one person of monastic ordination offering a butter lamp the size of a mustard seed.

In the same sutra it says:

> If all of those beings, transformed into chakravartins, were to fill the whole world with flowers and offer it, even greater merit than that—in fact hundreds of times greater than that—would be accumulated by one monastic offering one flower. In fact, the merit of those chakravartins would not be a hundredth or even a thousandth of that. Beyond that, if the monastic were motivated by bodhicitta, the merit would be even greater. Beyond that, if their motivation were embraced by non-conceptuality, it would be even greater still.

The Sutra of Piled Flowers says:

> Better than making offerings to or venerating in all appropriate ways a buddha for thousands of years would be to venerate a stupa after that buddha's parinirvana with bodhicitta as your motivation and offer flowers and incense or one lamp or one handful of water or say, "Homage to the Buddha." This is because even such slight acts of virtue motivated by bodhicitta will cause the person who does them to not pass into lower realms for a hundred thousand eons.

The Sutra of Piled Jewels says:

> If all sentient beings of the threefold world were to each create a stupa the size of Mt. Meru and serve it for a number of eons equal in number to the number of grains of sand in the river Ganges, there would be still more merit gained by someone with bodhicitta offering one flower.

The same thing is said in *The Sutra on the Appearance of Maitreya*.

In that way, in all of the Buddha's teachings and in the commentaries upon them the results of actions both to be done and to be abstained from are spoken of in detail. For someone who is actually able to follow this advice it is not necessary to repeat this. However, for the benefit of those who may not have understood it yet, again in the *Lotus Sutra* it says:

> Ananda, the perfect awakening that is accomplished throughout billions of eons is destroyed by three things. [*This doesn't mean you can destroy perfect awakening once it has happened, but it means future perfect awakening.*] If you ask what these three things are, they are lack of faith, not practicing, and absence of teaching.

In another sutra it says, "At the time when the Buddha's teachings are close to disappearing, even by teaching one sentence or one line of Dharma you will have served the teachings."

The Sutra on the Full Apprehension of Virtues says:

> At the time of the destruction of the teachings when it is difficult to practice them, if someone has respect for them and guards the teachings and upholds them they will be protected by all devas. They will be blessed by all buddhas and protected by them.

In another sutra it says:

> It is worse than engaging in the five actions of immediate consequence to incorrectly explain through misunderstanding the profound meaning of the Dharma. Therefore, in order to benefit the teachings one must explain them properly and in order to do so one must encourage others to engage in the training while engaging in training oneself.

In other words, what is called "upholding the teachings" means to engage in the training yourself and encourage others to engage in it. That will also establish householders in faith, which will cause what you teach to be meaningful.

In *The Eight-Thousand Stanza Prajnaparamita* it says:

> A bodhisattva who is taken care of by a spiritual friend will attain unsurpassable perfect awakening. Therefore, by guiding beings in the spiritual path you will fulfill the responsibility of a spiritual friend. It is important for those with discernment to consider this. As is extolled, do not promise what you cannot promise and do not break the promises that you have already made. To properly fulfill the requirements of the training taught by the Buddha in this way is utterly unlike the pretentious or fake practice of Dharma in the world.

The author of the text, the Ninth Situ Rinpoche, concludes this part by saying, "Since it has been written that it is permissible to rephrase the meaning of the teachings in a way that will be easily understood, I have summarized many of these quotations."

Finally, the text concludes in its entirety with a statement that it was written by Situ Rinpoche. This completes our study of the text *Rest for the Fortunate*, and of the practice of nyungne.

Bardor Tulku Rinpoche

Preparing for Death and the Bardo States

Introduction

When the topic of death and dying comes up, there is normally the tendency to react with great fear. The most important thing to understand at the beginning of such a teaching, though, is that we do not teach about it in order to inspire fear. Instead, these teachings are given so that we can come to understand the process of dying and what happens after death. By coming to such an understanding, and also through understanding the results of actions—that virtuous actions lead to states of happiness and negative actions lead to states of suffering—we will be able to prepare ourselves for death and ensure that we achieve a good rebirth after this life.

We presently enjoy an extraordinary form of life. As human beings, we possess eighteen different conditions which comprise the great freedom and precious resources of a human existence. The fact that we have and are enjoying these things now can only have resulted from our previously having gathered a great amount of merit. This means that in the past we have engaged in virtuous actions and abstained from negative actions, and especially that we have maintained flawless morality in previous lives. We have achieved the type of rebirth we enjoy now through our virtue in previous lives. In the same way, the only cause of a higher rebirth in the future is pure morality. Therefore, if we wish to achieve a higher rebirth in our future lives, we need to continue practicing moral discipline in this life.

Bardor Tulku Rinpoche

The Buddhist teachings emphasize that a human life is very hard to acquire, and also very easy to lose. This is to say that human life does not last forever. Our lives are extremely fragile. With that in mind, we should recognize that while we still have this human life, we possess the opportunity, the freedom, and the resources of a human existence, and thus we have the capability of accomplishing our own benefit. Going beyond that, we have the ability to cultivate a truly altruistic intention. If we can achieve that which is beneficial to ourselves and which is ultimately beneficial to others in this life, then we need have no fear whatsoever at the time of our death. That is why we talk about and study the process of dying and death and what happens after death.

Furthermore, although we tend not to remember it, this is not the first body or incarnation that we have experienced. It is said that the cycle of existence, or samsara, has been continuous throughout beginningless time. It is beginningless and endless, which means that we have been born and died innumerable times already. It is said therefore that if all the flesh of our previous bodies were piled up, they would make a mountain larger than any mountain in the world. If all the blood from our previous bodies were spread out, it would form an ocean larger than all the oceans of the world combined. Each time we have been born we have definitely died, since death always ensues at some point after birth.

Because we are obscured by our habitual patterns, we are normally unable to remember our previous lives. Not understanding that we have already been born and died an innumerable number of times, we are terrified at the prospect of death. We fear it because we do not realize that we have already experienced it innumerable times. For example, we do not fear going to sleep at night, because we can remember having gone to sleep and having woken up the next morning. Therefore, we can be fairly certain that we will wake up tomorrow morning when we go to sleep tonight. Since we cannot remember the process of dying and the process of being reborn, we fear death. We fear it in a way that is really no more necessary than fearing going to sleep and waking up the next morning.

The purpose of studying the process of dying, death, and the period after death, is to understand it sufficiently so that you can do two things. The first is to use the process of dying and death to achieve spiritual progress or enhancement yourself. The second is to understand it so you can help others through the death process, and in that way protect them from the suffering of dying and death.

There is further significance to the explanation of the process of death and dying, and this is the fundamental reason that all the buddhas and bodhisattvas out of great compassion have taught so much about the process of dying and death. This is connected with the fundamental nature of ourselves and of all beings. In the view of the mahayana tradition in general, as well as in the context of the mahamudra teachings, the nature of all beings is referred to as *sugatagharba*, or buddha nature. Essentially, buddha nature is the innate or inherent potential for awakening. In the context of an explanation of the experience of death and the bardo, this is called the ground clear light, or ground luminosity. It is called the ground luminosity because it is the fundamental ground of being and experience. This fundamental ground of being is the nature of the mind of each and every being, even the smallest insect.

While this ground luminosity is always the nature of the mind of each and every being, we do not normally experience it directly. It is, however, directly experienced by each and every being without exception during the experience of death. Unfortunately, we normally fail to recognize it, and therefore we do not achieve liberation merely through experiencing it. However, if we prepare ourselves during our lives for the experience of the ground luminosity, then when we experience it at death, we can achieve liberation through doing so. In the context of the bardo teaching, what we cultivate in our practice is called path clear light, or path luminosity. This consists of the entire process of practice that we undertake in the path of meditation in order to familiarize ourselves with the nature of our minds. Thus it includes the cultivation of mental stability (the practice of shamata or tranquility meditation); the cultivation of insight through the practice of vipasyana; the gathering of the conceptual accumulation of merit and the non-conceptual accumulation of wisdom; the practice of mahamudra; the practice of the generation stage (i.e., the visualization of deities); and the various practices of the completion stage as well.

The ultimate purpose of all these practices is to gradually familiarize yourself with your own basic nature. If you develop a familiarity with your nature such that it is sufficient to enable you to recognize that nature when it is directly experienced at the time of death, then that is called "the ground and the path, meeting like mother and child." Whenever a mother meets her child, even if the child is amongst hundreds of other children, she will still be able to recognize her own child immediately upon seeing it. In the same way, if you have cultivated a familiarity with your nature (which is called the path clear light and is like the child during your life), then as soon as the source of that, the fundamental or ground clear light (which is like the mother) is encountered at the time of death, the recognition — and therefore liberation — will be instantaneous. If you have cultivated sufficient familiarity with your nature to make this a certainty, then you need have no fear whatsoever of the experience of dying and death because, for you, death is not annihilation. Death is awakening. It is actually an opportunity to achieve the ultimate goal of all Buddhists. It is the reason that we pursue the path, and what we pray to achieve. Therefore it is said, "For the practitioner, death is not death, but awakening."

Another reason that it is inappropriate to regard the bardo state as a negative thing is the way it is experienced and used by enlightened beings. When an enlightened individual — for example, those who intentionally accept successive rebirths for the benefit of beings — passes away, we call it "passing into peace" or "dissolving into the dharmadhatu." What actually happens when someone who has achieved awakening passes away is that their mind dissolves into the dharmakaya, from which they arise in the form of a sambhogakaya buddha. They remain in the sambhogakaya until they start to produce the subsequent emanation of a nirmanakaya. For the period during which they are manifesting as the sambhogakaya, they benefit those with whom they have a karmic connection through the extraordinary activity of a sambhogakaya buddha. Therefore, this period after death, far from being a negative or tragic thing, is seen as their most victorious activity.

It should be noted that the term *bardo*, or interval, is used in different ways. It does not refer exclusively to the period after death, or even to the period preceding death. In many books that have been translated into the English language, you find extensive discussions of different numbers of bardos which make up the process of existence. For example, in *The Great Liberation Through Hearing in the Bardo*, which has been translated into English and is well known, six intervals are presented. These are: the interval between birth and death, the interval of dying, the interval of the dharmata or the nature of things, the interval of becoming or rebirth, the interval of meditation, and the interval of dream and sleep. Another well-known treatment of the bardo also available in English is the book *Mirror of Mindfulness* by Tsele Natsok Rangdrol. In this book, Tsele Rinpoche explains four bardos, namely the bardo between birth and death (also called the bardo of suffering), the bardo of dying, the bardo of the clear light (the bardo of dharmata), and the bardo of becoming, which is the process of rebirth.

Bardor Tulku Rinpoche

The Bardo Teachings of Guru Rinpoche

The text on which this present teaching is based is called *A Supplement to the Profound Meaning of Liberation Through Hearing*, which is a part of the *Cycle of Dispelling All Obstacles, the Accomplishment of the Heart of the Guru*. Most of the text was composed by the terton[21] Chokgyur Dechen Lingpa, and the quotations were composed by Guru Rinpoche himself.

The first thing we must understand about the view of dying and death presented here is that everything we experience or acquire during our lives, everything that appears to us, and everything that apparently exists surrounding us — no matter how wonderful, vivid, or abundant it may be — is utterly impermanent. When something changes from being what it is into being something else, or when it is destroyed or lost in some way, it vanishes as completely as the contents of last night's dream. Just as you can never recover the images of a previous night's dream, once something has been destroyed or changed, it is gone. Nothing that is composite (meaning that it results from the coming together of various causes and conditions) is beyond that. Nothing that is composite is permanent, nor can it remain unchanging.

Therefore, everything that we experience during our lives — including our very lives themselves — and everything that we have built up, will at some point be lost. Nothing is beyond what are called the four ends. The four ends are that: (1) all births must end in death; (2) all gatherings must end in separation; (3) all accumulation must end in dispersal; and (4) all creation must end in destruction. Whatever we have around us, and whatever we possess during our lives, we are definitely going to lose. Of all the things to which we become attached during our lives, that to which we are

---

21. A *terton* is a person who discovers hidden teachings known as *terma*.

the most attached is, ironically, that which is most fragile—our life itself. The life of any being—especially someone of our species, because humans have a very uncertain life span—is as transitory as a flash of lightning in the midst of the night. It is as fragile as a candle flame in a strong wind. It is as unstable as a bubble that appears on the surface of the water. Like these analogies, a human life is very brief and fragile.

What we call death is when this fragility, this impermanence of human life, finally manifests for us. It means leaving this world and going to our next form of existence. The first thing that needs to be understood about death is that although we become very concerned about death when it happens to us, we are by no means the only person to whom death has happened. Death happens continually to all human beings and to all beings in general. Once any being has been born in any form of existence, it is absolutely certain that this being is going to die once again at some point in time. If you look at it from that point of view—that death is the natural result or completion of the process of birth—you can see that there is no reason to be so unhappy about the idea or the fact of death.

Rather than being so unhappy or obsessively fearful about the prospect of death that you cannot even think about it, it would be better to focus one-pointedly in supplication of the sources of refuge—your teachers, the Three Jewels, and so on, those to whom you look for assistance—in order to go through the process of dying and death in the most positive way you can.

The second point that needs to be emphasized in the beginning is that, not only are you impermanent, but everything you have accumulated during your life will be lost when you die. All of the things you have accumulated, and all of the people to whom you are attached, will be lost to you when you die. You will never see them again in that form and they will not accompany you through the process of death. They can accompany you up to the moment of your death, but once you die, you are alone. You are going through the process completely alone.

Your possessions in particular cannot help you through the process of dying, and possessions most certainly cannot help you after you are dead. In fact, not only do they not help you, but they can cause you problems. This is the case because all of the things that you did in order to acquire those possessions, and all of the attachment that you have for those possessions and for everything you are leaving behind, can agitate you so much that it can make the process of death — and therefore the subsequent rebirth — much worse than it need be.

The Bardo of Dying: Dissolution and the Four Wisdoms

As we have seen, the different bardos can be categorized and presented in different ways. In this presentation they are divided into three, which are the three bardos that are aspects or parts of the process of dying and death. The first of these is the interval or period of dying — the experience of dying itself, which leads up to, but does not include the actual process after death. This is defined as the process or experience of the separation of your body and mind, which during your life have been integrated. The fundamental characteristic of the experience of dying is called the dissolution of the elements. In the text called *The Tantra of the Play of Wisdom*, it says:

> First, earth dissolves into water, water dissolves into fire, fire dissolves into wind, and then wind dissolves into consciousness. This consciousness, which apprehends, finally dissolves into the clear light.

These stages of dissolution occur when three things that sustain your life are exhausted or used up. The first is your vitality. Your vitality is basically the result of your previous accumulation of karma. In any case, when the vitality — the conditions that enable you to remain physically or biologically alive—is used up, then the elements that are the aspects of your physical living being start to dissolve. The second is the karma that has caused you to be reborn as, for example, a human being and has caused you to remain a human being for a certain length of time. The third is the merit that has kept you alive. Your life is maintained by your store of merit. When the particular store of merit that causes this particular life to last is used up, then the elements—the balance of which maintain your health and your life—start to dissolve.

What is meant here by the elements is the fundamental qualities of physical existence, particularly as they are found in biological life. What is called earth refers to the aspect of solidity of a living being. Just as our bodies are produced by the coming together of various physical causes and conditions, and our bodies therefore partake of the characteristics of the physical substance, our health is maintained by the proper balance of these physical characteristics.

At the time of death, there is the dissolution of these physical characteristics, one into another. The first step is that earth, which means solidity, dissolves into water, which is fluidity. This refers to the first stage of dying where your physical toughness or strength gradually diminishes. The second stage is that water dissolves into fire, and fire is, of course, your body's warmth. At this point, the liquid quality starts to dissolve. From the outside inward, the fluids of your body dissolve into the fire element. The third stage is fire dissolving into wind, or air. At that point the warmth of your body starts to be withdrawn inward. It leaves the limbs from the extremities inward, and gradually you become cold. The fourth stage is that wind or air dissolves into consciousness. That is the name for the point where you stop breathing. Our normal breathing is referred to as "external breathing," which means the type of breathing that could be detected easily by an observer. This breathing ceases at this point. The next stage of dying is called consciousness dissolving into space. At that point most, but not all, of the functions of your energy and mind stop. Your breathing stops altogether. Then the final stage is space dissolving into the clear light. That process actually has four stages within it, which are called "the arising of the four wisdoms."

During our lives, there is a channel at the very center of our bodies called the *avadhuti*, and within that channel there is a wind called the "wind of vitality." One of the things that this wind of vitality does is maintain the position of two fundamental constituents that link our mind and body together as a sentient form of biological life. One of these two constituents is identified with the original sperm from the father which fertilized the ovum. This is called the "white constituent" and is held in place by this wind at the top of our head. The other constituent is identified with the ovum of our mother. It is called the "red constituent" and it is held in place below the naval, at the bottom of the central channel, by this same wind. The wind of vitality keeps these two constituents (which are also known as "drops") separate. Through the process of the dissolution of the elements — in other words, through the process of dying up to this point — the energy or wind of vitality has withdrawn. As it withdraws, there is nothing keeping these two constituents in their previous locations, and their movement in sequence is what causes or precipitates the emergence of what are called the four wisdoms.

The first of the four wisdoms is called the *wisdom of appearance*. Through the cessation of the wind of vitality, the white constituent that was previously at the top of your head moves down through the central channel, finally reaching the center of your heart. While that is going on what the dying person experiences is that everything turns brilliantly white. That appearance of whiteness is why it is called "appearance." At the same time, as a cognitive experience, you experience a state of wisdom, a state of primordially pure awareness within your mind that is extremely lucid, but fairly free of conceptualization. Because your state of mind turns into that pure awareness, all of your aggression, aversion, hatred, and anger ceases. We have within us a great deal of aversion, attachment, and apathy. These three basic samsaric patterns are connected with how we take rebirth at the beginning, and they are maintained by us throughout our lives. At this point, though, the whole complex of emotions that we could categorize as aversion and anger ceases as this white drop reaches the heart.

The next stage, the second wisdom, is called the *wisdom of increase* (or augmentation). "Increase" refers to the red constituent moving up from below the navel until it, too, reaches the heart. When that happens what you experience in terms of appearance is that everything turns bright red. That is called the appearance of increase. At the same time, as a cognitive experience, you experience a wisdom that is even more intense than the previous one. You experience a wisdom that is not only lucid, but also blissful and pleasant. There is a tremendous sense of well-being. The cognitive lucidity and the well-being are not two different things. They are the same thing, although we describe them in two different ways. Because of that intense experience of well-being that emerges out of the lucidity at this point, all attachment and desire cease. Whereas previously all aversion ceased, in this stage all attachments and desires cease because they have become irrelevant.

Eventually these two constituents or drops meet together at the heart. At that point, the third wisdom arises, which is called *attainment*. This is the point where if someone has led a very, very negative life, they may become extremely terrified. Basically what happens here is that the person becomes unconscious briefly. As they become unconscious, they experience everything turning into utter darkness. It is not like a small amount of utter darkness, but an endless expanse. The cognitive experience that accompanies this darkness is that the wisdom becomes even more intensified. It is not only a wisdom characterized by well-being and lucidity, but it is also utterly non-conceptual, free of any kind of thought. At that point the klesha of apathy ceases. We normally do not recognize apathy, but up to this point it is constantly present in our lives.

Next, the fourth stage or wisdom ensues upon the third. At this point, the person has momentarily become unconscious. It is like blacking out for a moment. All of this happens much more quickly than it takes to describe, which is the problem with the description. It sounds as though we are talking about a very gradual process that you could witness comfortably. It is not like that, however.

As we have seen, through this process of dissolution, all our usual types of reactivity (attachment, aversion, or apathy) have simply dissolved into space. Because all of this has dissolved into space, then the moment after that the fourth situation arises, which is a completely pure wisdom called *perfect attainment*. This is the ground clear light.

At this point, what is experienced is the fundamental nature of your mind — buddha nature. Buddha nature is that naked, simple awareness, which is aware without any conceptualization or thought of the present moment of experience. In the language of the tradition of this instruction, it is called "a self-arisen, primordial awareness that is pure from the very beginning." In and of itself, it is free from any kind of impurity, any kind of conceptualization. It has no defect. It is not missing anything and does not require anything being done to it, anything being removed from it, or anything being added to it. It is perfect just as it is. It is utterly unpolluted by any kind of attitude, state of mind, or cognitive process. This is what you experience at that fourth moment. Every being experiences it at this point in the process of death, but they would never be able to describe it.

However, if through the process of practice during your life you have familiarized yourself sufficiently — through meditation practice and so on — with the nature of your mind so as to be able to recognize it at this point, then you achieve buddhahood. This is the dharmakaya as the ground.

There is nothing to be afraid of if you have assurance that you can achieve buddhahood in the dharmakaya at the moment of death.

To illustrate this, a quotation is given from the teachings of Guru Rinpoche about this process and the state with which it ends. He says:

> Fortunate children of good family [*i.e., of the mahayana*], listen with undistracted mindfulness. All of the appearances of this world, whatever they are and how many they be, are like dreams — like the illusions or the seductions of a deceiver — in that all of them are impermanent. All of them are destructible. Therefore, let go of suffering, attending upon their loss. The appearances during the processes of dying — the whiteness, the redness, the blackness — all of these appearances are the display of your own mind. There is nothing in any of this that appears to you that is something other than yourself. Therefore, children of good family, be not afraid, be not terrified. And at the culmination of these, when it seems that you become unconscious, and that your awareness fails you, externally you perceive an appearance that is like a clear sky, and internally your cognition becomes like a lamp burning inside a vase. It is lucid, but utterly non-conceptual, and naturally remains, one-pointedly. This is the clear light that arises at the time of death, and this is the wisdom of all buddhas. Rest in this, relaxed, without attempting to alter it, without attempting to change it. If you do so, you will be liberated in the dharmakaya.

At this point the process of death is complete. The person has died. Therefore that is the end of the first of the three bardos, the bardo of dying.

In discussing the first of the three bardos associated with the experience of death, we have seen how, if you have gained sufficient familiarity with the nature of your mind to be able to recognize the ground clear light when you experience it after death, you can attain liberation at that moment in the dharmakaya. This is how liberation can be attained in the first bardo, the bardo of dying. If, however, you do not attain liberation in the bardo of dying because you do not recognize the fundamental or ground clear light, then the second bardo will arise. This is called the bardo of dharmata or the bardo of the nature of things.

The Bardo of Dharmata: The Peaceful and Wrathful Deities

The second bardo, the bardo of dharmata, consists of the experience of what is called "spontaneous presence." This is the spontaneous expression of the qualities of the ground, in the form of the peaceful and wrathful deities, light, rays of light, and so on. It is the display of the goodness of the ground itself, manifesting in this form. In general, the opportunity for liberation in this bardo consists of not being overwhelmed by the brilliance and majesty of the display, and especially recognizing that all of this light and all of these deities are nothing other than the display of your own awareness. In brief, it means recognizing that these are simply the display of the inherent qualities of your own buddha nature. They are not in any way external to yourself. If in the second bardo, you can recognize the appearances that occur as the display of your own mind and rest calmly in that recognition, then you will attain liberation in the sambhogakaya. In the first bardo, the opportunity is for liberation in the dharmakaya. In the second bardo the opportunity is for liberation in the sambhogakaya. This is explained in more detail in the words of Guru Rinpoche:

> The first experience of death is the experience of the ground clear light, and if you do not recognize that awareness — because the ground clear light is your own fundamental awareness — then for a period of seven days after that, you start to experience certain visions or appearances. Throughout this period of the

bardo of dharmata, everything that you see, everything that appears to you, is like rainbow light, which is to say that it is brilliant five-colored light and rays of light. Amongst this light and rays of light are spheres or droplets of brilliant five-colored light. Within these you see the forms of various deities. All of this—the five-colored light, the rays of light, the droplets and so on—are the display of the five buddha families, that is to say, the five buddhas. They arise as a display before you because they are aspects of your own buddha nature. They are inherent within you. The wisdom, the inherent or innate wisdom of your own buddha nature, manifests at this point, apparently external to yourself. During your life, these things are within you. They are within your channels, winds, and drops. Normally you do not experience them directly or visually, because you have a body. After death, your mind having separated from the body at this point, or at least being within the body, but not being biologically seated in it, these things can be experienced. The light and the rays of light that you see in the bardo of dharmata are so bright and powerful that you find them threatening or frightening. You want to run from them. The usual reaction a sentient being has at this point in the bardo is to try to escape from all of this brilliant multi-colored light. What is recommended here is not to be frightened of this light, but to recognize it as being your own display. In other words, it is the light of radiance of the inherent qualities of your own nature.

At the same time you see all these rays of brilliant multicolored light, you see other lights that are much dimmer, and much more comfortable. They are much more appealing. They are more like what you would want. They are the degree of brightness you would choose naturally if you could choose light. The standard reaction a sentient being has is to run away from the bright light and to be attracted to, or be drawn to, the muted light. However, the muted light is the display of your five poisons (kleshas). The muted light, which is comfortable and familiar to you, is the path that will lead you into rebirth in samsara. Therefore, just as you need to not be frightened of the brilliant lights of wisdom, you also need not to be seduced by the muted or comforting light of the kleshas. This is the point where you actually visually see the choice between wisdom and confusion, or nirvana and samsara, in the form of brilliant light and muted, comforting, soft light respectively. This is the point, as it says in the text, where you have to *not* make the wrong choice.

Within all of the brilliant light, you see the forms of the five male and female buddhas. Along with all of the other rays of brilliant light, rays of light emerge from the hearts of the five buddhas, and these enter or strike your heart and eyes. That is called "the great secret path of Vajrasattva," and it is the point where you have the greatest opportunity to achieve liberation. It is also the point where you are likely to be the most frightened or threatened by the deities, because not only are these rays of light everywhere, but they actually seem to be shooting towards you as though they were going to pierce you in some way. If you recognize that these lights and these deities are not other than yourself, and especially if you can supplicate them with sincere devotion, saying something like, "Take hold of me with your compassion," you will attain liberation in the sambhogakaya. If you can supplicate them rather than running away from them, and recognize that the deities are not other than yourself, simply just remaining with that, without attempting to do anything, without feeling that there is anything in the situation that you have to get rid of or anything that you have to add — simply by resting in that, the deities will start to dissolve. At that point, because you did not run away from them, you will attain liberation in the sambhogakaya.

That is the first half of the bardo of dharmata. It is called the peaceful bardo, or the bardo of the peaceful deities, because as threatening as the displays of light, rays of light, and so on may seem to be, up to this point they are nevertheless peaceful in appearance. The deities — the buddhas of the five families — appear as peaceful male and female buddhas.

If you do not attain liberation in the sambhogakaya at this point, then the appearances of the deities will change. The nature of the situation itself has not changed, however. The deities themselves are not changing, but your perception of them changes. Whereas previously you saw extremely brilliant (and therefore somewhat frightening) but otherwise beautiful rainbow light everywhere, now above, below, and all around you the rainbow light starts to be tinged with a light that is like fire. It becomes an endless expanse of five-colored flames of wisdom. The deities that you see at this point are extremely wrathful in appearance. Again, there are the five female and five male buddhas, but their appearance is transformed from being peaceful and smiling into being extremely wrathful and threatening. These are the rest of the deities who are spoken of in the bardo. Normally it is said that there are forty-two peaceful and fifty-eight wrathful deities who appear. These wrathful deities have all sorts of different appearances, and they are quite terrifying. They are holding lots of different sorts of ghastly weapons, and they are laughing in a very, very threatening way, exclaiming sounds like the mantras *Hung*, *P'ey*, and so on. They are blazing with light and flames that are even more intense than those of the previous deities.

Again, this is a further opportunity for liberation — and again, the same response is necessary. You need to not be frightened of them. These deities are not in any way threatening. They are again a display of your own wisdom, just in a particularly intense form. Recognizing that all of these deities are simply the display, the appearance, of your own awareness, and being certain of that, then just simply stay put. Simply rest in that, without attempting to flee. Especially at this point, rather than attempting to run away from them, if you can actually mix your mind with the mind of the wrathful deities who appear to you, then you will attain liberation in the sambhogakaya.

If you do not attain liberation in the sambhogakaya while experiencing the second bardo, it is due to the habit of dualism. It means you are conceiving of these deities that appear to you as separate from yourself. Because you are holding onto your mind and your being as inherently different from the appearances of those deities, then you do not attain liberation in the sambhogakaya. In other words, it is through a fixation on the appearance of duality that this liberation may not be attained.

The Bardo of Becoming: The Journey of the Consciousness

If you have not attained liberation at this point, then the third bardo begins. This bardo begins with your consciousness exiting your body. Previously, of course, you had died, so your consciousness was no longer functioning in your body the way it did when you were alive. However, it was still remaining within the center of your heart. But if you do not attain liberation at the end of the bardo of dharmata, then the consciousness will leave your body at that point. At that point your consciousness will, in your perception, take the form of your previous body. The appearances of the bardo of becoming, this third and last phase of the bardo, are explained in the *Abidharmakosha* as follows:

> Your form appears to be that of your previous life, and can be seen by similar beings and those with the divine eye. You possess karmic miraculous powers. Your senses are complete, and you can move without impediment, without being stopped. This is the form of a *gandharva*.[22]

You do not actually have a body at this point, but your consciousness, which has now exited your previous physical body, appears to you to take the form of that body. Because you are used to looking a certain way, you assume you still

---

22. Gandharva is a name that is given to several types of etherial beings, including beings in the bardo states.

do. A bardo being at this stage can be perceived by other bardo beings, and by individuals who have attained the divine eye of being able to see bardo beings and so on. Possessing karmic miraculous powers does not mean that you have the genuine miraculous powers that arise from meditation. However, because you do not have a body, you have what we normally would regard as the miraculous power of being able to move anywhere in an instant just by thinking of it. Although that is the case, it is not under your control, which is why it is called "karmic." What happens is that you think of a place and all of a sudden you are there, whether you want to be there or not. No time elapses in traveling there.

Regardless of whether all your senses were functional in your previous life, this mental body appears to have complete senses. It appears to be able to see, hear, smell, taste, and feel. You feel hunger and thirst, but the sustenance you want is smells. The bardo beings are called gandharvas, or "smell consumers." If you take food that is consecrated to the benefit of bardo beings in certain ways and you singe or burn it, the smoke from that can actually nourish them. This is why in the period of time (usually forty-nine days) after someone's death we often perform this kind of burnt offering where food is singed and dedicated to those beings.[23] They are actually nourished by it. They consume it just the way we would, and feel a sense of well-being from that, just as we would from eating food.

Throughout this forty-nine day period, you seem to have the body that you had in your last life. It will probably appear more or less the way it appeared toward the end of your life. As well, you will experience an uncertain and bewildering variety of other appearances. You think of a place, and you find you are there. Many of these appearances can be frightening, and you experience a great deal of anxiety

---

23. This practice is called a *sur* in Tibetan.

and even terror because you feel that you are being threatened by things. You feel that you are going to be burnt by a fire or drowned by water. You think you are about to fall off a precipice or be crushed by a boulder, or other things like that. The correct approach to this bardo is to regard whatever appearances that arise as unreal, as illusory, and in that way you do not react to them. In traversing this bardo, you need to resist the tendency to react emotionally to the appearances that you experience — to be attached to some, averse to others, and apathetic about the rest. You need to regard whatever you experience as the display of emptiness. Regard everything as being without any substantial existence. As well, you need to try to preserve an outlook of compassion. These are the most important things. If you can earnestly preserve a recognition of the emptiness of the hallucinations or appearances, and an attitude of compassion, this will help a great deal.

The other thing needed here is renunciation for samsara, because the bardo of becoming is the point where you start to be impelled toward taking rebirth. Therefore, at this point it is important to recollect that wherever you might be reborn in samsara, in whichever of the six realms, it is going to be an experience that is fundamentally one of suffering, without any true or complete happiness at all. During this bardo, in addition to recognizing emptiness and maintaining compassion, if you have the thought, "I must, at all costs, attain liberation from samsara," that is very important. If you have renunciation for samsara, you will not be compelled to be reborn in the same way you would if you lacked such renunciation.

In addition to the attitude of renunciation through feeling sadness for samsara, during this bardo you need to supplicate those in whom you have the greatest faith — your teachers, the Three Jewels, and so on, and you need to generate the intention to take rebirth in a pure realm. A pure realm here means a pure nirmanakaya realm — the realms of the five buddha families. In particular, it is recommended to aim for the pure realm of the Buddha Amitabha. Because of Amitabha's aspiration, it is very, very easy to achieve a rebirth in his realm simply through wishing to be reborn there. Especially at this point in the bardo, through hearing the name of Amitabha and through wishing to achieve a rebirth in his realm, you can actually achieve it. The goal in this third bardo is to achieve rebirth in the realm of Amitabha. Therefore, at this point, along with emptiness and compassion, renunciation, and supplication of your teachers and the Three Jewels in general, bring to mind Amitabha and the qualities of his realm, Sukhavati (Dewachen in Tibetan).

It is also important that your intention for wishing to be born in Sukhavati is a compassionate one. To be successful, the intention needs to be the thought that, "In order to be able to liberate all beings from existence, I wish to be reborn in Sukhavati." If you have bodhicitta as your motivation, it is quite possible to achieve this. Through these attitudes on your part—the aspiration to rebirth, compassion, bodhicitta, and so on—and through the truth of dharmata, through the blessings of your teachers, and especially through the momentum of your aspiration at this point in the bardo, you will achieve rebirth in the natural nirmanakaya realm of Sukhavati.

This part of the bardo is discussed in the following quotation by Guru Rinpoche:

> At this point in the bardo you are experiencing the appearance of a body that is actually just your basic energy and mind which are inseparable. It is not a physical substance. In that mental body what you experience are the unstable appearances of the bardo of becoming.

If you have not attained liberation already—in other words, if you have reached this point—you probably did not know you were dead until now. Now, however, you figure it out. You realize that you are dead. Your natural reaction to this, of course, is to miss very much those you left behind and to yearn for them, which can be a problem for the dead person. At the same time, you may have some hallucinations of things being out to get you. You feel pursued. It is somewhat individual, but you will have some hallucination of something, or some things, being after you. You will hear things that will frighten you, and in general you will be quite scared.

The experiences in this phase of the bardo are of two types. Some are standard, which is to say that basically everyone experiences the same things. Some are individual, according to your own particular makeup. However, whatever you see and whatever you hear, you must recognize that it is all the display, the projection, of your own mind. Being the projection of your mind, it is of the same stuff as your mind and your mind is empty, like space. Therefore, none of these projections can do anything to you. All you are is a mind, with no substantial physical existence whatsoever. Therefore, it cannot be hurt. No matter what you think you see coming after you, what you hear and so on, none of it can hurt you. In fact, none of it actually exists. It is all just projections or hallucinations of your mind. Remind yourself of that at this time in the bardo, and generate a courageous confidence of recognizing the nature of what is occurring.

It is traditional to prepare a *sur* or burnt offering for the deceased during this phase of the bardo. They can actually be nourished by it, because beings experience hunger and thirst at this time, and what they want are smells. Usually there are blessing substances mixed in with these which also affect them beneficially and make it possible for them to attain liberation. The most important thing that the person needs to be reminded of, or that the person needs to remember, is not to be obsessively concerned with what they left behind, but to direct their minds in an attitude of supplication to those in whom they have faith—their teachers, the Three Jewels, and so on. It is especially important to recollect the existence of the realm of Sukhavati. In other words, it is essential not to try and get back to the life you left, but to move on, and especially to move on to Sukhavati, which is experienced by beings in the bardo as being located in the western direction. Moving west, they move toward Sukhavati. Buddha Amitabha resides in the midst of that realm, and at this point in the bardo anyone who supplicates him by name can achieve rebirth at will in his realm. The text addressing the deceased says:

> Recollecting his name, pray to him. Ask for the assistance of Avalokiteshvara and Padmasambhava. Generate devotion and if you can do so without doubt, in an instant, you will find yourself in the realm of Sukhavati, born instantaneously in the calyx of a lotus.

In this way, the deceased is instructed not to be depressed about the fact that they have died — which they are just coming to terms with — but to be delighted because they have the opportunity to achieve rebirth in a pure realm.

Taking a Positive Rebirth

If you think back to what we have discussed so far, three different opportunities for liberation have been described: the opportunity for liberation in the dharmakaya during the bardo of dying; the opportunity for liberation in the sambhogakaya in the bardo of dharmata; and finally the opportunity for liberation in the nirmanakaya by achieving rebirth in a pure realm in the bardo of becoming. Obviously, however, not everyone attains liberation during any of these three stages. Therefore, the next thing presented is what to do if you are in the bardo of becoming and you have not achieved rebirth in a pure realm.

At this point, since you are going to be reborn, you have to choose an appropriate rebirth, one in which you can progress toward liberation. As has been said, during your time in the bardo of becoming you have possessed a mental body that looked like the body you had in the previous life. Now you are getting closer and closer to entering your next place of rebirth and therefore you start to experience your body appearing as what it is going to be in your next life. For example, if you have the karma to be reborn as a preta or hungry ghost, your body starts to change into a preta body, with a very, very narrow neck and an extremely big belly and so on. If you are going to be reborn as a deva or god, then you start to experience your body as a deva body, and so on.

At the same time, you start to perceive the environment that you are moving toward, the one into which you are tending to be reborn. As you approach the entrance into that realm, which in the case of the human realm is the time of conception, you actually see the parents. In the case of a rebirth which involves parents, such as human or animal rebirth, you will generally see the parents. This is the point at which you can do something to control where you are reborn. The reason you can do something is that the actual proximate cause of your being conceived is the attitude you take towards the parents. Without taking a certain pair of attitudes, you will not enter into the womb, or enter into the union of the parents. Basically, if you are going to be reborn as a male, you will feel attachment and desire for the mother, and aversion and aggression towards the father. If you are going to be reborn as a female, you will experience attachment for the father and aversion for the mother. Therefore, if you can stop these kleshas from arising, you will not be pulled into the rebirth. In not being motivated by kleshas, the rebirth that you take will be motivated by your positive aspirations.

Since at this point you actually see your prospective parents, a very effective way to stop the kleshas is to transform your perception of the parents into a pure perception. Instead of regarding them as being just male and female human beings, or whatever other kind of beings they are, regard them as male and female deities — your particular deities, whichever ones they are. You can also regard them as male and female gurus. For example, if you are someone who meditates upon yidams such as Chakrasamvara, Gyalwa Gyamtso, or some form of Guru Rinpoche, then you can view the parents as these. That will stop your generation of an attitude of obsession with the parents which would cause you to achieve rebirth unwillingly. At the same time, making the aspiration to be born to parents who will enable you to progress further on the path of Dharma will cause that to happen. Since you are not being pulled into rebirth through kleshas, then the force that comes into play is your positive aspiration. The primary function of this is to prevent your being reborn in lower realms, so that at least you can achieve a human rebirth, and especially to achieve a human rebirth through which you can progress further along the path.

At this point in the bardo, since you have not yet stopped the process of rebirth by attaining liberation, you start to see the environment in which you are tending to be reborn. It could be something like the rotted stump of a tree or a dark cavern, or it could be a forest. On the other hand, it could be a magnificent palace. It all depends upon whatever rebirth you are heading toward. The first thing you have to do is let go of any attachment or craving you have for the environment, because no matter how unpleasant the environment is from our point of view, at that point in the bardo, if you have a karmic compulsion to be reborn there, you are going to be attracted to it. Make the aspiration to be born in this human realm, and especially in a place where genuine Dharma has spread, and be born in a situation such that you can receive guidance from authentic teachers. Make the aspiration to be born to parents who will encourage or facilitate your spiritual growth. To do this you can regard any parents that you seem to be moving towards as the father and mother guru. Our source text refers to "father and mother Guru Padmasambhava." That is because the text was written by Guru Padmasambhava, but it could be any deity with whom you are familiar. That will enable you to let go of attachment for one parent and aversion for the other, so that the motivating force that propels you to rebirth is your positive aspiration, not compulsion. You will be able to rest in meditation through faith, and by doing this you will then be reborn in a situation such that you will be a receptacle for the profound Dharma, and will quickly attain liberation.

These are the four stages of instruction concerning the profound possibilities of liberation at the time of death and soon thereafter. We have seen how it is possible to achieve liberation in the bardo of dying, in the bardo of dharmata, and in the bardo of becoming, and then if you do not achieve liberation at those opportunities, how to achieve a positive rebirth in the bardo of becoming. The instructions are presented sequentially, so that if one does not work, you do the next one, and so on. This ensures that if you learn these instructions during your life and familiarize yourself with them, regardless of how confused and ignorant you may think you are, you will definitely achieve liberation within seven lifetimes. These instructions are so powerful that if you learn them, or if they are actually spoken to you after your death, you can achieve liberation through them, even though you may not have been the most heroically diligent practitioner during your life.

QUESTIONS AND ANSWERS

Question: I believe you said that life comes to an end when the merit associated with that life is used up. Is that true for bodhisattvas who have chosen to reincarnate in this world?

Rinpoche: Not really. The presentation we have gone through is really about what happens to a normal being. There are two types of beings who do not experience the bardo at all. One type is an awakened person who does not go through these kinds of experiences because they have already fully awakened, so the process is not one of any kind of loss of control. They do not experience what we would normally call the bardo at all. The other type of person or being who does not experience the bardo is someone who has been so viciously harmful to others that they have turned their state into one so profoundly negative that the whole thing just happens very, very quickly. They do not have a bardo at all. They just basically proceed to hell. For most beings, however, it happens in the stages we have been discussing.

Question: How much do you have to practice to accomplish this recognition after death?

Rinpoche: It depends upon your own degree of insight. There are people who have so much receptivity that when the nature of their mind is pointed out by their guru, they recognize it on the spot and they do not need to practice at all—ever. If that does not happen, then really the only answer to that question is to say that the benefit will be in accordance with however much you practice and study.

Question: If someone falls into the state of hell, do they ever find their way out, or are they there eternally?

Rinpoche: They do not stay there forever. Nothing is forever. However, they stay there until the karma that caused them to be reborn in hell is used up, which could take a very long time.

Question: I have often heard that at the moment of death people have a life review, an experience in which their whole life passes in front of them. I was wondering where something like that fits into the four dissolutions, or if that is not something that is taught in the Buddhist system.

Rinpoche: That probably happens after the death process is over and you are in the bardo. When you are in the bardo after death, your awareness is said to be many times more lucid than it was during your life, so you can remember everything that you did.

Question: Would someone going through a near-death experience go through the same process as someone who is dying?

Rinpoche: According to this tradition, a near-death experience is a partial experience of dying. The appearances that you undergo in a near-death experience are basically the same experiences as those in the dying process, except that at a certain point it stopped—you did not go all the way. This brings up the question as to exactly how far you can get in this before you are at the point of no return. According to these texts, if you remember the sequence of dissolution we went through, you can get up to, but not including, the point that is called consciousness dissolving into space. The external breathing could stop, but internally there is still going to be some warmth about the heart. There is still something that is not completely shut down, and at that point the person can possibly be revived. However, if they actually experience the appearances of white, red, and so forth, which are the experiences that a person goes through when they really go all the way through the death process, at that point there is no turning back.

Question: In the reports on near-death experiences, people do say that they see a white light. Would that be different than what you are talking about here?

Rinpoche: It would not be what is called the radiant appearance. It is probably one of the appearances of the dissolution of the elements, which occur earlier. That stage is possible to experience and still come back. You can go through the dissolution of the five elements, and that process also has different kinds of things that you see and so on, so the reports of near-death experiences are probably one of those. No one has ever been able to come back and say what the radiant white appearance is like, because when you go that far, you are going the rest of the way.

Question: Do the stages of dissolution all the way into the four wisdoms always take the same length of time, or is it slower or faster in different kinds of death, or with people with different levels of realization?

Rinpoche: The duration of each stage of the dying process is uncertain and depends on how you die. If you die suddenly, such as through a sudden violent death where you lose consciousness very quickly, you go through all of this, but you go through it in a split second. That is why it is considered so important for someone who is a practitioner to have a very tranquil death, if possible, so that nothing interferes with their consciously going through the process of dying, and so that they might be able to recognize the ground clear light.

Question: Do the four stages that occur after you are beyond the point of no return also take place faster or slower depending on the type of death?

Rinpoche: Yes, very much so. In a violent death, for example, these stages would happen very quickly.

Question: Do all beings go through this experience, or is it only those in the human realm?

Rinpoche: We tend not to recognize it, but all beings will experience this, not just humans.

Question: When I was watching my mother die, I noticed that her limbs got extremely cold, starting at the feet and hands. As she approached death, her breathing became labored and she eventually stopped breathing. At that point I noticed her whole body was cold with the exception of the crown of her head, and a portion of her heart. That remained warm for some time, until the coroner came and then, of course, I had to leave. But up until that point, which was probably a good hour, it was still warm. Is that a physiological phenomenon, or could you say that the consciousness was dissolving into space?

Rinpoche: It is very difficult to say, but generally warmth being present in a certain part of the body indicates that the person's consciousness has not yet left the body. This is very important in the case of performing the ejection of consciousness (*powa*[24]) for the deceased. There is a distinction between the consciousness being *present* in the person and its being *seated* within their organism. If the consciousness is still in the body, and if in fact it is still biologically seated in the body, then technically the person is not yet dead. By ejecting their consciousness at that point, when it is still seated within their organism, then they are still not dead, and by performing the ejection of consciousness you would be killing them. Therefore the transference cannot be done at that point. If someone were present who was going to perform the *powa*, they would determine, based on various signs, if and when the consciousness had departed.

Question: Could that be the case even though the person had stopped breathing and were pronounced dead by a medical doctor?

---

24. Powa is a practice of transferring a being's consciousness to Dewachen. It can be performed by oneself prior to death, or by a qualified person for someone after they have died.

Rinpoche: There are a lot of things that have to be examined to see exactly where someone is in this process. There is a standard diagnostic procedure at that point. The various arteries, veins, and so on have to be checked. In the case of a person who actually has a realization of the nature of his or her mind, this warmth will last around the heart region in particular not only for an hour, but sometimes for days or even weeks. In that case, we would have to say that technically the person is deceased, but nevertheless they are not completely done with their bodies yet, because the complexion does not deteriorate the way it normally does after death. It does not become mottled or pale. In fact, in such cases the complexion generally looks better than it did while the person was alive. That remains, and the warmth in the area of the heart — which you can feel by touching them there — remains for this period. Then when their consciousness has left the body completely, they start to look like a corpse. Another way you can check for this state of meditation is that normally if you pinch or distend a dead person's flesh in some way, it will stay the way you have pressed it. It will stay pinched, because it does not have the elasticity of living flesh. In the case of someone who is remaining within this meditative absorption after death, the flesh of the body responds like living tissue.

Question: Are you saying that even though the person has stopped breathing, the heart has stopped, and he or she has been pronounced dead by a physician, that all these other phenomena can still take place, and the consciousness could still be remaining in the body?

Rinpoche: The person is actually dead at that point, but because they are resting within samadhi the consciousness has not yet left the body.

Question: For a highly realized being, when they have died and perhaps even taken on another body, is there some aspect that remains particular to that incarnation — some form, even though they may have taken on another body? For example, I know people who have seen Kalu Rinpoche. Even though he has taken on another body, there are aspects of him that seem to have remained from his previous incarnation.

Rinpoche: That is an instance of their being able to display whatever form is going to be most beneficial for a particular being. In the case of someone who is going to be more benefited by having, for example, a vision of their appearance from a previous incarnation, then they will have that vision. That being or teacher will manifest to that person in the perceived form of a previous incarnation, or whatever form is going to be the most beneficial. For those who will be the most benefited by direct, ordinary contact with the present incarnation, the teacher will manifest in that form. The fact that they might choose to appear to someone in the form of a previous incarnation does not mean that there really is a difference between the nature or effectiveness of the previous and subsequent incarnations. It is simply a necessary concession being made for our fixation with appearances. Having become accustomed to their having a certain appearance, we identify that appearance with them, and therefore we are more receptive to it. We might have more faith in it. Because we would be more open to blessing in that form, therefore they would appear in that form. However, it is only a concession to our fixations.

Question: I have heard it said that when a being dies there is a period of some days when the consciousness stays in the body, and during that time it is best if the body is not disturbed. Could you comment on that?

Rinpoche: The period for this is normally said to be three days. Again, this is different from the case where someone is remaining in samadhi. Then the amount of time is actually uncertain. It can last for a long time. The reason for this three-day period is twofold. One reason is that normally when someone dies, they may — although they are dead and their mind is no longer biologically seated in their body the way it was when they were alive — their mind may stay in their body for a few days. The other reason is that even if it does not, they may not realize they are dead for a while, and they may therefore identify very much with the body. If the body is disturbed when they do not yet realize that they are dead, they can get quite angry. And the anger that they generate at seeing what is done to their body can negatively impact the process of rebirth for them. For that reason, it is traditionally recommended to leave the body undisturbed for three days. Nowadays, however, this is almost impossible.

Question: I am concerned that nowadays many people are heavily sedated or drugged at the time of death, primarily to ease the pain. I am concerned that this might affect their proper experience of dying.

Rinpoche: First of all, the use of painkilling drugs is an entirely different situation from giving them something to actually kill them, to hasten their death, which is something else. If they are given medication to ease the pain, that will either not affect the situation, or it will help. The reason it can help is that the worst thing — the most distracting thing — is going to be extreme pain. Therefore, the reduction of the person's pain during the process of dying will make them much more able to recognize the dissolution process than they would be in the midst of pain.

Question: You mentioned that there are certain kinds of experiences from which a person cannot return to describe, because they have gone too far to come back. If no one has come back from beyond that point, how do we know about these things?

Rinpoche: There are three ways that we know about this. The fundamental way is that the Buddha taught about it. The second way is that there was a phenomenon in Tibet which was called *delok*, which is considered to be different from a near-death experience. People would actually go all the way through this, really die, and after up to a week or more come back to their bodies. Because of what they undergo, this is considered to be different from someone being in a coma and waking up. The proof of the difference lies in what the person could describe about the bardo and other things that they saw. And deloks—which means people who really died and came back—are able to give very accurate and consistent descriptions of the dying process. They are a second source of information about this. Then the third source—although it is uncommon—is people who, especially in early life, remember their previous death and bardo experience.

Question: I have heard that there are directions called "pointing out" that can be given which enable one to directly recognize the nature of the mind at death. Could you comment about that?

Rinpoche: I cannot give those instructions in this context because it is our tradition to only give them when someone has completed what are known as the preliminary practices, or *ngöndro*. The ngöndro practice is a set of what are called the common and uncommon preliminaries. The common preliminaries are the four thoughts which turn the mind to Dharma, and the uncommon preliminaries are four sets of intensive meditation practices. You can find out about these in the book *The Torch of Certainty* by Jamgön Kongtrül the Great. These preliminary practices are in themselves quite an extensive subject, so I would not be able to go through them here in detail.

Question: If an animal is hit in the road and they are in excruciating pain and you come upon them, is it alright (even though it is difficult) to end their life so they are not in extreme agony? The other question concerns humans if they are terminally ill. It is not an easy transition if they are in constant pain. Is it ever permissible to assist somebody in dying? Let's say there is somebody in your own family who is in constant pain and there is just no medication to help with that—is there ever a time when you can help them to end their life?

Rinpoche: It is actually the same situation whether you are talking about an animal or a human being. In either case, it is taught that you should not kill them. What we call assisting death is killing. For example, in the case of an animal that has been hit by a car and you find it on the road suffering tremendously, the almost instinctual wish to "put them out of their misery" is based upon the mistaken idea that by killing them you are going to end their suffering. The only thing you are ending by doing that is your having to watch their suffering; you are not ending their experience of suffering. If their life is ended unnaturally through your action, then the karma that is causing them to experience that suffering has not been dealt with. This means they are still going to experience it, and it is probably going to be much worse. Therefore, although you may not be able to get rid of all their suffering, you simply have to do what you can to alleviate it without killing them. You can also do other things to help them, for instance, before they die or immediately after their death you can recite in their ears the names of buddhas as well as mantras such as those of Amitabha and Avalokiteshvara. The same thing is really true for human beings as well.

Question: How does the taking of one's own life affect the process of death and subsequent rebirth?

Rinpoche: Killing yourself is no better than killing anyone else. Karmically it is the same thing. You accumulate the karma of killing by killing yourself, just as you would by killing any other being.

Question: In the third bardo, is the mind different from the mind that we have now? When you were talking about it I was feeling anxiety, because it felt like being in a dream state, and when we are in a dream state we can't help reacting, and I was wondering if the mind or the consciousness is different in the bardo than it is now.

Rinpoche: No. Your mind is not unclear or intoxicated the way it is in a dream. In fact, it is clearer than it is now. Of course, dreams vary. Some people's dreams are very, very vague and their minds are very unclear, and other people have very clear consciousness during dreams.

Question: In this teaching, it seemed like you were talking about the mind as a thing in itself, whereas I have heard it described as being like a stream.

Rinpoche: You can call it a continuum or stream if you want to, but the mind is not a "thing" in the sense of being a substantial entity. The problem with leaving it at that is that we may then assume that the mind is nothing at all. It is no more "nothing" than it is "something," because while your mind has no substantial existence whatsoever, it nevertheless is the cause of your falling into samsara, and the cause of your achieving liberation from samsara. Therefore it is said, "The mind is not 'something' because it is not seen, even by buddhas, but the mind is not 'nothing,' because it is the ground or starting point of all samsara and nirvana." However, saying that it is not something and not nothing is not contradictory, because the mind cannot be conceived of in those terms.

Question: I am concerned that, if I died right now, how I could get somebody, maybe a lama like yourself, to come and do those prayers over my body. I am not really well-practiced at this point, so in order to be liberated I would need somebody to help me. How could I do that? Who would help me?

Rinpoche: The most important thing is not so much whether an external person such as a teacher and so on is there with your body to say these words to you or not. The most important thing is that within yourself you have certainty in your understanding of this process of death and bardo. That means having the confidence of a clear understanding of what is going to happen, and in that way being prepared. It is especially important that you have faith in the sources of refuge—the Buddha, Dharma, and Sangha—because they will never let you down. If you depend upon an external person such as myself, then you are putting yourself at risk, because, who knows, I might die first, and then you would be left stranded. The way this is explained in this text and in other texts of instruction about dying and death is that the best way to prepare yourself is to practice enough meditation — that is, tranquility (shamata) and insight (vipasyana) — that you familiarize yourself with the nature of your mind. If you succeed in doing so, you have no need of any external individual to remind you, because you are familiar with it and then you simply recognize it. If you cannot do that, then the particular approach taken within Tibetan Buddhism in general, which is based upon the vajrayana tradition, is to attempt to mix your mind at death with the mind of your guru, based upon the confidence that your guru is the embodiment of the Buddha, Dharma, and Sangha. If you have a certainty and confidence in your guru such that you can mix your mind with his or her mind, then the physical presence or absence of your guru is irrelevant.

Question: What if I do not have a guru at this point?

Rinpoche: Well, if you do not have one, then you might think about gradually looking for one. If you do not actually ever find one, then you can direct your mind to the Three Jewels — the Buddha, Dharma, and Sangha.

Question: I would like to know what our local Buddhist community should do if one of the members of our group dies. Are there particular rituals or responsibilities of the sangha when that happens?

Rinpoche: It is definitely good to do something as a sangha when someone you have known personally, or a member of the sangha, passes away. What we do at KTD is that whenever anyone passes away, for at least forty-nine days after their passing, butter lamps are offered in the shrine room in front of the images of the Buddha and deities, with the merit of that being dedicated to their wakefulness in the bardo. Also the community is invited to participate in special ceremonies for them. These generally consist of performing the Chenrezig and Amitabha practices, more or less as usual, except that they are specifically dedicated to that person's welfare. It is not always practical to have that going on for the whole forty-nine days, but special observances take place at least for some period of time, and regularly during the period. You could do the same thing wherever there is a center and a community of practitioners. It is also excellent to request the prayers of great awakened teachers when someone dies.

Question: If this type of thing is done for people who are not Dharma practitioners—let's say our relatives, friends, or people we may know who are not part of the Dharma—how is it that this is helpful to them, when they have no apparent connection?

Rinpoche: It still helps, regardless of their belief system, because essentially when you do these practices you are actually praying for all beings, for the benefit of all beings. You are cultivating an attitude that is completely altruistic and positive, and then you are dedicating the virtue and goodness of that attitude to the benefit of the deceased. Regardless of the deceased's belief system, it still is going to have a positive effect on them. A distinction needs to be made, however, between the prayers you might say for someone after they have passed away and things you might say to them before they pass away. If someone who is dying has a strongly held belief system—for example, let's say they are devoted to a religion other than Buddhism, exclusively, and are not particularly receptive to Buddhism—you should obviously not go to them at the point of their death and say, "Now, direct your mind to the Buddhadharma" and so on, because it is going to upset them. But it is not going to upset them after their death if you are praying to Amitabha and Chenrezig for their benefit. People's attitudes change after death based upon what they are experiencing. Also, whether they believe in karma or not, karma still affects them, and can be used to benefit them.

There is a story in the sutras about two of the Buddha's closest disciples, the Arhat Maudgalyayana, who was the greatest performer of miracles among the Buddha's disciples, and the Arhat Shariputra, who was the wisest of the Buddha's shravaka disciples. At one point, through their miraculous powers, they travelled to a certain hell realm. There they encountered a being who had previously been a non-Buddhist teacher, someone whom they had known when he was alive. After his death he had been reborn in this hell realm. His followers believed that in order to ensure a positive rebirth after someone's death, the best thing to do was lots of animal sacrifice. That was part of their religion. Every year on the anniversary of his death they would get hundreds and hundreds of animals and slaughter them. Therefore the being who was now in hell said to Maudgalyayana, "When you go back up there, you must tell those people to stop doing this, because every time they kill all these animals it just makes my situation much, much worse." They went back to the human realm, and Maudgalyayana tried to tell the followers of this teacher that what they were doing in commemoration of his death was causing him unbelievable suffering. But they were so angry at what Maudgalyayana was claiming about their teacher that they did not listen, and beat him up instead.

Question: What types of beings are the ghosts that people sometimes see? Are they bardo beings?

Rinpoche: The ghosts that people see are not necessarily beings in the bardo. They could actually be experiencing a type of incarnation that is called pretas or hungry ghosts in the Buddhist tradition. This is one of the six realms of samsaric existence.

Question: When a being takes rebirth in the pure realms, is that the end of cyclic existence for them?

Rinpoche: In a sense, yes. Once someone has been reborn in a pure realm, such as that of Amitabha, they will never again be reborn in samsara. On the other hand, this does not mean that being reborn in the pure realm is like a permanent vacation of some kind. The precise name for these realms is "natural nirmanakaya realms," but normally we call them pure realms. When you are reborn in one of these pure realms, from the moment of your birth, things are quite different from what we know. For example, you are born in the sense that you just appear in the midst of a blooming lotus flower. Immediately upon birth there, you are already a bodhisattva. I said that being born there is not exactly a vacation because the purpose of being born there is to progress through the rest of the path until you finally attain buddhahood. Once you attain buddhahood there, you do what all buddhas do, which is to engage forever in nonconceptual activity for the benefit of beings. The activity of a buddha is different from ours in many ways, but the most obvious way is that whenever we do anything, we have to plan it. We have to think about it. We have to decide what we are going to do and what we are not going to do. We have to think, "Well, I will help this person, and then I will help that person, and I will do this by buying that," and so on. Buddhas do not have to think. It just kind of happens automatically. That is the final result of being born in a pure realm.

Question: Could you talk about what the Amitabha practice entails, how frequently it should be done, and if it is good to do it individually as well as in a group?

Rinpoche: The Amitabha practice can be done either as a group or individually. You can also do either the long or short form of the practice. The short form is the one that is normally done after the Chenrezig practice at KTD and in the centers. If you do not perform one of the complete practices, then you can simply recite his name mantra, *om ami dewa hri*. The most important thing, which is more important than what form of the practice you do, is that you amass what are called "the four causes of rebirth in Sukhavati." If you are aiming to be reborn in Sukhavati, the realm of Amitabha, whether or not you will be successful depends upon these four things. The first cause is called the recollection of the realm. This means to think regularly, or frequently, about the appearance of Amitabha and his retinue—the Bodhisattvas Avalokiteshvara and Vajrapani and so on. You think about the existence of this pure realm and bring it to mind often. The second cause is to accumulate as much merit as you possibly can. The third cause is to generate bodhicitta, which is to say to generate the aspiration to establish all beings without exception in a state of buddhahood. The fourth cause is to dedicate whatever virtue you accumulate to the rebirth of all beings without exception in the realm of Sukhavati. If you accumulate these four causes, then there is no doubt whatsoever that you will be reborn in Sukhavati, because it is not really accomplished through your own power or spiritual attainment. It is accomplished through the aspiration of Amitabha.

Question: For someone you know who has died, is it a good thing to read the translation of *The Tibetan Book of the Dead*?

Rinpoche: It would be helpful, but the most important thing when reading it is that you read it correctly, which means without mistakes. It should be read such that the listening bardo being can understand what you are saying.

Question: *The Tibetan Book of the Dead* has specific days mentioned to read specific things, and there is always mentioned the forty-nine days after death. Does the bardo of becoming always take the same period of time for every being?

Rinpoche: There is the common custom that has developed of praying for and commemorating the person who has died for forty-nine days, which is fine. But we should not assume that everyone's bardo state is of that duration. The actual duration of the bardo is somewhat individual because in the sequence of events that are said to take one week, and so on, the days are not days of ordinary time. The days are not solar days. They are known as "meditation days." A meditation day is the length of time an individual can rest his or her mind without distraction. Thus in the text when it says something like, "And then for the next seven days everything will appear as rainbow light," seven days does not mean a calendar week. It means seven times the amount of time that the particular being in the bardo can rest their mind without thought.

Question: You spoke about the bright light in the bardo as compared to the duller light, and that some beings are more comfortable with the duller, more mundane light. Could you talk a bit more about the bright light? Why would a bright light be so frightening?

Rinpoche: The reason that the brilliant rainbow light and the deities and so on which appear within it are so frightening is not really something inherent in the quality of the light itself. It is very, very bright, but the bardo being is terrified of it because of his or her own tendencies and reactivity, not because there is something objectively present in the light that we would call inherently scary. There are many reasons they should *not* be afraid of this light, the most obvious one being that they do not have a body, so what are they worried about? There is nothing for them to be afraid of. The light cannot do anything to them, and the deities cannot do anything to them — not that they would anyway. Nevertheless, the habit of fear is so strong that we react that way, even though there is no reason whatsoever that we should. It is just like the way people react to the sight of a snake. Some people see a snake and run. Other people see a snake and pick it up by the head.

Question: What kind of person would *not* be frightened of the light? In other words, what characteristics should we cultivate and develop in this lifetime, in order not to be frightened?

Rinpoche: The person who will not be frightened is the person who knows what it is that they are seeing. And the person who will be frightened is the person who does not know what they are seeing. To use the example of the snake again—if you see a snake, and you do not know whether it is a poisonous snake or not, you are going to be very frightened. But if you see the snake and you know exactly what kind of snake it is and you know it is not poisonous and there is nothing to be afraid of, you are not going to be frightened. Therefore, the more you know about what to expect in the bardo, the more familiar you are with what you are going to experience, and the less you are going to be frightened of it.

Question: When you encounter the deities, if you do not run away and if you supplicate them, what happens then? Do they dissolve, or do they dissolve into you?

Rinpoche: Basically what happens is that you remember that the liberation in the sambhogakaya really occurs through recognizing that the deities are not separate from your own mind. Thus, the recognition of the deities as not being other than your own mind dissolves them as something separate or external. You can think of it as them dissolving into you, or you dissolving into them. It does not make any difference. It is the recognition that they were never outside you to begin with.

Question: You mentioned that the consciousness stays with the body for some time after death, and goes through a couple of stages before it then leaves. Is there a period during which the body should be left completely alone? Should it not be embalmed or cremated or whatever during a period to allow this consciousness to remain within the body?

Rinpoche: Traditionally in Tibet, people would always keep the body undisturbed for three days, and if they had the means and opportunity to do so, for forty-nine.

Question: My understanding is that most people do not recall their previous lives, and I have heard that even tulkus frequently do not. Why is remembering the previous life so very difficult?

Rinpoche: The fundamental reason we do not recollect our previous lives is that when your consciousness gets connected with the physical substances which begin the process of gestation and eventually birth, it is almost like becoming drunk. It is like the way a substance going into your body alters your consciousness; it is like getting intoxicated or bewildered by the mind's getting mixed up with these substances. This creates an experience of discontinuity so that there is usually no recollection of the previous experience. That is the reason for ordinary beings.

With regard to tulkus recollecting previous lives, when they say they do not remember, you should take it with a grain of salt. For example, if you went up to His Holiness the Gyalwa Karmapa and you said, "Do you remember your previous lives?" he would say, "Of course not." But you have to think about whether that might be true or not. This is someone who — forget about remembering previous lives — remembers his future lives! Before he passes away, he gives the names of his next parents, the location of his birth, and other details, so that it will be easy to find him. He has done this consistently. He also recognizes other tulkus immediately when he is asked to find them. If he can do all of that, obviously he remembers his own previous lives as well, but out of modesty he is going to tell you that he does not.

Question: Since Amitabha practice is so strongly connected with death and dying and rebirth in Sukhavati, could you discuss that briefly? In particular, could you briefly describe the role that the empowerment ceremony plays in connecting us with the practice?

Rinpoche: The function of the empowerment of Amitabha is to introduce the blessing of the lineage of this tradition into your practice of Amitabha. In order to achieve rebirth in Sukhavati, you need to accomplish the four causes that I explained earlier. If you accomplish these four causes, you will achieve rebirth there. In Tibetan Buddhism, a tremendous amount of emphasis is placed upon the continuity of the succession, or lineage, which is the basis for the authenticity of the teachings. This means that before you do any practice, you have to receive the blessing of the lineage of that practice, which depends upon receiving three things. The first is called the empowerment that ripens or matures, and the second is called the instruction that liberates. The third is the reading transmission, which is sometimes called "the reading transmission that supports, or forms a container," and sometimes, "the reading transmission that bears blessing."

The function of an empowerment is therefore to ripen your buddha nature, almost like watering a plant. You have an innate potential for awakening, and the function of empowerment is to help it emerge. Any practice you do, though it is virtuous, will not have the same authenticity or the same power as it will if you receive the transmission of the lineage through empowerment, reading transmission, and instruction.

Rinpoche's conclusion: The main point that I want to leave you with is to continue to practice. Whatever your present practice may be, the fundamental and ultimate aim of such practice is to cultivate the familiarity with our mind's nature that is called the path clear light or path luminosity. The point of doing so is that at the moment of our death we can recognize the ground or fundamental clear light, and achieve liberation. Always remember that this is the aim of your practice, whatever specific form it may take along the way.